TO   FROM

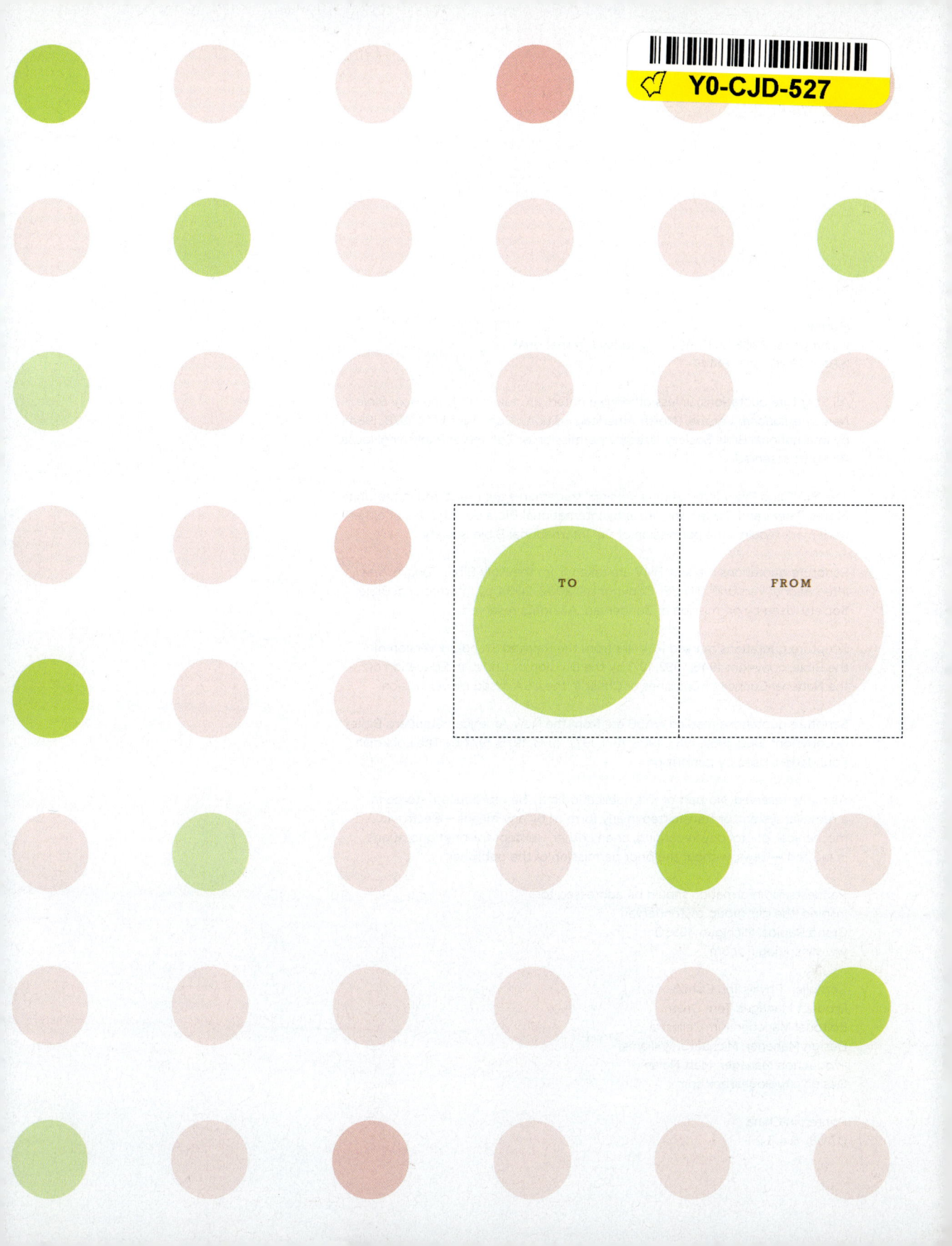

Renew
Copyright © 2006 by Christianity Today International
ISBN 978-0-310-81446-7

All Scripture quotations, unless otherwise noted, are taken from the *Holy Bible: New International Version*, (North American Edition). Copyright 1973, 1978, 1984 by International Bible Society. Used by permission of ZondervanPublishingHouse. All rights reserved.

The "NIV" and "New International Version" trademarks are registered in the United States Patent and Trademark Office by International Bible Society. Use of either trademark requires the permission of the International Bible Society.

Scripture quotations marked TNIV are taken from the Holy Bible, *Today's New International Version*®. TNIV®. Copyright © 2002, 2004 by International Bible Society. Used by permission of Zondervan. All rights reserved.

Scripture quotations marked RSV are from the Revised Standard Version of the Bible, copyright 1946, 1952, 1971 by the Division of Christian Education of the National Council of Churches of Christ in the USA. Used by permission.

Scripture quotations marked NASB are from the New American Standard Bible, © Copyright 1960, 1962, 1963, 1968, 1971, 1972, 1973, 1975, 1977 by The Lockman Foundation. Used by permission.

All rights reserved. No part of this publication may be reproduced, stored in a retrieval system, or transmitted in any form or by any means — electronic, mechanical, photocopy, recording, or any other — except for brief quotations in printed reviews, without the prior permission of the publisher.

Requests for information should be addressed to:
Inspirio, the gift group of Zondervan
Grand Rapids, Michigan 49530
www.inspiriogifts.com

Compiler: Phyllis Ten Elshof
Product Manager: Tom Dean
Editorial Manager: Kim Zeilestra
Design Manager: Michael J. Williams
Production Manager: Matt Nolan
Design: studiogearbox.com

Printed in China
07 08/ 5 4 3 2 1

renew.

a devotional magazine for women

contents

Chapter One: Health and Beauty
- Makeover with a Mission
- Extreme Makeover
- Freedom with Age
- Easing Up on Externals
- Holy Workout
- Walking to Audio Books
- Changing with the Change
- Finding God's Heart
- Outpacing Depression
- Winning Against Breast Cancer

Chapter Two: Growing in God
- Power in Short Prayers
- Postures of Prayer
- The Blessings of Cancer
- Prayer Connection
- Traveling with Jesus
- Jump-start Your Quiet Time
- Hope in Loss
- A Caring Church
- Mentoring Donna

Chapter Three: Rest
- A Good Sabbath
- Enjoying Sunday
- Sleep to Your Health
- Getting Enough Sleep
- Sleep Problems in Marriage
- Give Stress a Rest
- Fighting Workaholism
- Unplugging Entertainment
- Practicing Peace
- Backyard Vacation

Chapter Four: Entertainment
- Taking Your Dream Trip
- Finding God in Travel
- Keeping Life an Adventure
- Praying through the News
- Tuning Out TV Marriage
- Homecoming after Vacation
- My Best Friends
- Fun for Two

Chapter Five: Home and Hospitality
- Helping Homesick Kids
- Entertaining Strangers
- Gift Giving
- Gardening for Missions
- Welcoming New Neighbors
- Making Friends around the Block
- Finding God in a Mobile Home
- Cleaning out the Clutter
- A Beautiful Bedroom

Chapter Six: Safety
- Comfort in Uncertain Times
- Safe for Life
- Working through Turmoil
- Finding Peace as a Hostage
- When God Takes the Reins
- Saving a Friend from Abuse
- Safe at Night
- Meeting a Guy Online
- Dan and the Motorcycle
- Keeping Teens Safe

Chapter Seven: Leaving a Legacy
- The Gift of Financial Order
- Transforming Guilt into Glory
- Legacy of Love
- Journal of Thanks
- Turning Loss into Celebration
- My Mother's Faith
- Model Grandma
- Tabitha's Legacy

Chapter Eight: Money
- Hope During Unemployment
- The Missing Check
- Giving Before Getting
- Enough for Retirement
- The Big Picture on Giving
- A New Approach to Tithing
- The Joys of Leaner Living
- How I Curbed Excess Spending

Chapter Nine: Transitions
- Becoming Parents Again
- Nestling into the Empty Nest
- Lessons of a Lay-off
- Finding Worth as a Widow
- Moving Again
- Tips for Changing Careers
- Growing Together in Retirement
- The Bible on Retirement

Chapter Ten: Personal Growth
- Keeping the Dream Alive
- Speaking Out on Corporate Infidelity
- Freedom from Workaholism
- Controlling Anger
- Chains of Opportunity
- Serving Where Called
- Freedom from Secrets

Chapter Eleven: Love and Friendship
- Rekindling Romance
- Lessons from My Pagan
- Light for the Dark Times of Marriage
- Serving Your Spouse
- Living with Irreconcilable Differences
- Spirit Lifters
- Keeping in Touch
- Forty and Single
- Sharing the Word
- Comfort Verses

Chapter Twelve: Family
- Burden of Blessing
- Intrusive Mother-in-Law
- Adopting as a Single Mom
- No More Children for Me
- My Sister and Friend
- Lester's Game
- Taking My Daughter to College
- Making New Traditions
- Parenting a Prodigal
- Enjoying Adult Daughters

CHAPTER ONE **HEALTH & BEAUTY**

makeover with a mission

As I approached a significant birthday, I realized I'd been neglecting my body. I'd gradually allowed busyness to replace time for exercise and daily devotions, and the resulting fatigue affected me physically and spiritually. So I decided to commit to a program of personal rejuvenation based on Scripture:

Psalm 119:11 TNIV "I have hidden your word in my heart." I began reading the Bible daily and memorizing verses.

Psalm 139:14 TNIV "I praise you because I am fearfully and wonderfully made." Each day I exercised at least one-half hour, doing floor exercises to stretch and flex or walking one or two miles.

1 Corinthians 10: 13 TNIV "God will not let you be tempted beyond what you can bear." Instead of giving in to the temptations to overeat, I now chose to eat smart. I fill up on water, fruits, or vegetables and limited myself to two thousand calories per day.

2 Samuel 22:26 "To the faithful you show yourself faithful." When I began my fitness program, I opted to weigh myself monthly rather than daily. I diligently pursued my weight-loss goals and soon felt thinner. But when I stepped on the scales, confident that I'd lost weight, I hadn't.

I could have been defeated by disappointment and disgust, had weight loss been my only goal. But it wasn't; I was rejuvenating the Holy Spirit's temple.

So I remained faithful to my new fitness routine. Gradually, I've lost fifteen pounds and gone down one clothing size. Although my body makeover is ongoing, I feel stronger and healthier. More importantly, I'm assured of God's faithfulness.[1]

"I TURNED MY INNER SELF OVER TO JESUS CHRIST, THE GREAT SURGEON WHO CAN MAKE OVER EVEN THE HARDEST CASES, AND HE TRANSFORMED MY PERSONALITY AND SPIRIT."

EXTREME MAKEOVER

Cynthia Culp Allen encourages women to care for their bodies without spending too much time or money. She and her daughter, Charity Allen Winters, remind women that the majority of our time and attention should focus on our spiritual life. In their books, Allen and Winters use their expertise and personal experiences to guide women toward a Christian perspective on physical beauty.

Allen, who competed in several beauty pageants when she was younger, has worked with supermodels and other women as a beauty consultant since 1973. Winters is a professional model and actress.

Allen says she is an example of an extreme makeover, though she has never been under the knife. "Yes, I've studied beauty and know how to care for my skin, hair, and body, but the makeover I'm speaking of, the one I share in our books, is the inner transformation that the Holy Spirit took me through in my college years," she says.

Allen says she struggled with low self-worth, depression, fear, negative thoughts, and was even suicidal before she experienced an extreme makeover. "I turned my inner self over to Jesus Christ, the Great Surgeon who can make over even the hardest cases, and he transformed my personality and spirit," she says. "When people hear my story, they can't believe it because I am so full of joy and confidence now.

"I guess that's the appeal of the Extreme Makeover show," she adds. "They take someone and make him or her into someone entirely different. That's what Jesus Christ does for us; he makes us new creations."[2]

"I am fearfully and wonderfully made." —Psalm 139:14 TNIV

Each day I exercised at least one-half hour, doing floor exercises to stretch and flex or walking one or two miles.

H_2O IS ESSENTIAL FOR GOOD HEALTH.

"I GUESS THAT'S THE APPEAL OF THE EXTREME MAKEOVER SHOW," SHE ADDS. "THEY TAKE SOMEONE AND MAKE HIM OR HER INTO SOMEONE ENTIRELY DIFFERENT. THAT'S WHAT JESUS CHRIST DOES FOR US; HE MAKES US NEW CREATIONS."

HEALTH & BEAUTY

"IT'S LESS ABOUT ME MAKING THINGS HAPPEN AND MORE ABOUT TRUSTING GOD WITH WHATEVER HAPPENS. IT'S ACCEPTING THE WAY THINGS ARE, AND LETTING GO OF THE THINGS THAT NEVER WILL BE."

Freedom with Age

At age forty, I wrote, "Gray hair gives you permission to be chemically dependent."

Girl, was I *ever*! Forty was the year I went seriously red. My motto was, "Why be salt-and-pepper when you can be paprika?"

At age fifty, I threw out the spice cabinet and discovered—whoa!—*my own natural hair color*.

My hairdresser nearly fainted when I asked her to take the silvery color at my roots and weave it through the rest of my hair. I went silver in two hours instead of two years.

Oh, the freedom! No more worries about my roots showing or pricey trips to the salon or attempts to match my makeup to my hair color of the month.

I now have a whole palette of natural shades, each one chosen by the Lord, whose Word reminds me, "Gray hair is a crown of splendor" (Proverbs 16:31). Personally, I prefer the word *silver*. Rather than coloring my hair, I now polish it.

At age forty, I wrote, "The pressure is off."

Who was I kidding?! Like many women, I spent my thirties and forties trying to raise children and build a career at the same time. Whew.

At age fifty, the pressure really *is* starting to ease. My teens are now my role models. I watch them love their friends unconditionally and take the Bible seriously. And I no longer think of my work as *career*, but rather as *ministry*. It's less about Liz making things happen and more about trusting God with whatever happens. It's accepting the way things are, and letting go of the things that never will be.

It's peace with a capital P.[3]

EASING UP ON EXTERNALS

Before I was a Christian, having great looks and the right weight was preeminently important because that guaranteed my career and my ability to pick and choose the jobs I wanted.

But at age thirty-eight, for some reason, I feel my mortality. I can no longer control my body in terms of trying to look like it did in my twenties.

As a model, of course, I make my living on my looks; it's a big part of who I am. As I age and lose some of those looks, I'm discovering that I have to rely more on the inside Kim and the eternal Kim. Before I was a Christian, that was scary. Even as a Christian it's scary. But I've been maturing inside and out.

Growth doesn't always come easily. For example, when my husband and I travel to New York City, part of me wants to jump back into that New York scene, not in a bad way, but in wanting a new outfit so I can look a certain way. Or I'll meet a bunch of people and be impressed by them versus being impressed with God.

There are always little things from which you have to pull yourself back, evaluate, and say, "Ooh, no."

It's a constant battle.[4]

holy workout

STRENGTH TRAINING HELPS PREVENT OSTEOPOROSIS, BUILDS MUSCLES, INCREASES ENDURANCE, AND ENERGIZES YOU. IT CAN ALSO BECOME A HOLY ACTIVITY WHEN YOU SEEK TO GLORIFY GOD IN IT, TAKING GOOD CARE OF THE EARTHLY BODY THAT GOD ENTRUSTS TO YOU.

If you'd like to start strength training but are unsure about how to start, talk to your physician first, particularly if you have health concerns such as high blood pressure, heart disease, or diabetes.

Take time to learn about strength training from a trustworthy source; a local health club or YMCA is a great place to begin. Most health clubs have staff available to teach you how to use weight machines. Take time to learn proper technique to avoid injury. Consider hiring a certified personal trainer who can teach you the correct form for each exercise and offer a personalized fitness plan for you.

You might also check out www.acefitness.org, the American Council on Exercise website that provides guidelines for finding a reputable trainer as well as other resources.

You don't need to invest in expensive home-gym equipment or a health-club membership to reap strength-training benefits. You can work your upper body (biceps, triceps, shoulders, chest, and back) with soup cans, which weigh about a pound each. Squats, lunges, stomach crunches, and push-ups can also be done at home.

When you start exercising, pace yourself. If you do too much too soon, you'll pay for it with unbearably sore muscles over the next several days. A little soreness is okay, but start slow. Once you learn the basics and gain confidence, you can advance to a higher level. Allow forty-eight hours of recovery time between strength-training sessions. Never lift more than three times a week per muscle group.

Don't forget you need a cardio workout too. Your heart and lungs, as well as your muscles, will thank you if you treat them to generous doses of aerobic exercise.[6]

When you start exercising, pace yourself. If you do too much too soon, you'll pay for it with unbearably sore muscles over the next several days.

WALKING TO AUDIO BOOKS

My lack of physical fitness alarmed me. I knew I needed exercise, but every sport seemed either too hard or too boring. I couldn't run long enough to play tennis. I was bored when I tried to lift weights. I flailed around helplessly in an aerobics class. Was there a sport for someone like me, who was really out of shape? Was there an exercise for someone who'd rather be reading?

Finally, I prayed about it. "God, this is hopeless," I confessed.

One day I pulled up to our house and sat for a few minutes in the parked car, listening to an audiotape of Pride and Prejudice. I didn't want to turn off the tape, but I didn't want to spend the rest of the afternoon in the driveway, either.

I thought of how my brother put on headphones before he jogged down the beach. I couldn't possibly jog, but I could walk. I dug out a portable cassette player, popped in Pride and Prejudice, and tried walking around the block. I listened to Mr. Darcy snub Elizabeth Bennett at a ball. *Poor Elizabeth!* I thought, heaving myself up a hill. *She's too poor to ever marry!* Before Elizabeth had time to get back at Mr. Darcy, I had walked two and a half miles.

Since then, audio books have motivated me to get out the door for a daily walk. Sometimes, if I'm in the middle of a good book, I'll pass my house and keep going an extra mile or two.

Over the past eight years, I've listened to scores of books. My energy level has gradually increased, and my body has grown stronger. Recently after an aerobics class, I sat for a few minutes in the car, astonished. Since when could I keep up with an exercise class? How did I, the person who dreaded workouts, ever get into reasonable shape?

God gives us some miracles immediately; others can be seen only when we look back after we've gone a few hundred miles.[7]

CHANGING WITH THE CHANGE

THE START OF MENOPAUSE MARKED A GOOD TIME TO STARE DOWN MIDDLE AGE AND FACE MY FEARS ABOUT AGING. I CHOSE TO DO THAT BY GETTING SOME CHRISTIAN COUNSELING. I BEGAN TO EXPLORE MIDLIFE ISSUES SUCH AS: HAVE I BEEN A GOOD WIFE AND MOTHER? HAS MY LIFE BEEN WORTHWHILE? COULD MY MARRIAGE RECONFIGURE ITSELF WITH JUST TWO OF US IN OUR EMPTYING NEST? WAS I STILL DESIRABLE?

buy a harley

take naps

get fit

my widowed, never-married, childless, or divorced middle-aged girlfriends shared some of these issues, but they were also struggling with another heart-wrenching concern: the very real fear of loneliness or of never having had children.

These questions—often more troubling than actual physical symptoms brought on by menopause—are a key part of The Change. Still, the answers this season of life eventually provides can be a pot of gold at the end of the hormonal rainbow. God directed me to a skilled counselor as well as to numerous books by Christian psychologists that helped me cut through a lot of mumbo-jumbo about menopause proposed by non-Christians and gave me hope about getting through it.

Since I saw a number of my peers wilting at this stage of life, I decided to head full tilt into it. I followed an older mentor's example and bought a Harley-Davidson. I got a treadmill and began using it. I revamped my wardrobe, makeup, and hairstyle, peeling off a few extra years and infusing myself with confidence.

I wasn't shy about telling my husband and family what I was going through, and that helped them become more supportive. I purposely deleted energy-robbing responsibilities, including some church and Bible study, from my calendar. I added naps to my to-do list, and bulked up on complex carbs and low-fat proteins, dropping ten pounds in the process.

But most importantly, I sought out friends, both old and new, who had youthful, positive attitudes plus wise spiritual values. They helped convince me that I could make an eternal impact for God's kingdom before, during, and after menopause.[8]

> **While we may never understand** all the reasons behind God's decision to physically heal one person and not another, we can be assured that our pain is not meaningless to God.

FINDING GOD'S HEART

When my friend Paulette was dying ten years ago, I wanted to do something, anything, to make her well.

I thought I heard God telling me, "If the entire congregation gathers around her and prays, then I will heal her. If you fast for three days, then I will heal her." I thought I had found the key that would open the door to her healing.

So when Paulette died, I was disappointed with God. I had expected Him to deliver if I believed, prayed, and fasted. Deep down, I thought God was emotionally detached from Paulette's suffering and the pain we endured in watching her die. I couldn't believe that her death was God's will.

Jesus prayed fervently in the Garden of Gethsemane to be released from the pain of crucifixion (Matt. 26:39). He had done no wrong, but God still said no. God had an eternal purpose for his Son's pain. It was no little thing for our compassionate God to let his Son suffer. Yet God was willing to allow Jesus to suffer unspeakable horror so we could be forgiven of our sin and be reconciled to God.

Through the death of my friend Paulette, I've learned that God isn't a vending machine. We don't always get what we want, no matter how fervently we pray for it. Sometimes God heals; sometimes he doesn't (Ecclesiastes 3:1, 3). Ultimately, Jesus modeled the right attitude in prayer by surrendering to his Father's plan. He said, "Not my will, but yours be done" (Luke 22:42 TNIV). Like Jesus, we should pray that God's wil shall be done and give glory to God no matter how he answers.

While we may never understand all the reasons behind God's decision to physically heal one person and not another, we can be assured that our pain is not meaningless to God. One day, we, like Jesus, will rise victoriously, and our sorrow will be turned into joy as we all become one (John 17:20).[9]

OUTPACING DEPRESSION

I had been exhausted for months. I slept long hours every night and during the day as well. At any given time of day or night, I found myself able to sit on the couch, close my eyes, and drop immediately into the deepest sleep.

I wasn't sure what was happening to me. All I knew was that something was terribly wrong.

Around that time, I made an appointment to see a family doctor in our area, hoping he might recommend some vitamins to help me feel better. Instead, he said the magic words that brought both terror and hope into my life: "You're clinically depressed."

He then handed me a prescription and gave me some advice: "Exercise for half an hour, three to five times a week.

As much good as the medication will do, the exercise will do that much or more."

Depression is a scary word. Yet a wave of relief surged over my numb and exhausted spirit when I heard it. My enemy had a name. And if it had a name, maybe it had a cure. I felt the first stirrings of fragile hope. Maybe I could lick this thing yet.

I wish I could say that during my depression I spent hours in prayer, but the truth is that I felt too numb to pray. I remember sitting in my parked car one night and sobbing, "Jesus, I can't take it anymore. You've got to do something. I don't care what or how, but you've got to help me, please!"

Other than that, I felt too wounded to pray. Through this, I know now that Jesus hears us even when we're hurting too badly to say the words.

Late one night I stepped onto the back porch to feed our golden retriever, and I suddenly had the urge to run. Our house sits on an acre, and the backyard is bordered by evergreens. Chased by the dog, I ran toward the trees. The moon, hung like a silver earring in the sky, illuminated my crazy path as I ran. I stopped and watched my breath hang misty and white before me. I smelled promise in the air.

That was the first time I knew, really knew, that I was going to be okay.[10]

Depression is a scary word.
Yet a wave of relief surged over my numb and exhausted spirit when I heard it. My enemy had a name. And if it had a name, maybe it had a cure.

Winning Against Breast Cancer

Several years ago, Betty Rollins wrote a book titled *First You Cry*. I agree—there definitely is a time for tears when you learn you have cancer.

You cry on the elevator ride from the doctor's office after he's put you at the top of his hit list for surgery. You cry when your husband wraps his arms around you, trying to ease the blow of a biopsy report. You cry on the phone when you're telling your kids you're having a mastectomy. You cry when Mom tells you, "I wish I could have this instead of you."

But there's also a time to stop mourning and get back to life. One way to do that is to get back to whatever it is God has called you to do.

Work is therapeutic, I've found. It focuses attention on what you can do rather than on what you're powerless to control. It helps you feel productive and useful. And if you're as blessed as I am with believing coworkers, it plugs you back into a network of daily support.

But the best way to beat back the enemy is to put every fear into the hands of the God who made us, sustains us, and controls whatever happens to us. He knew I'd have cancer. In his unfathomable wisdom, he allowed it to happen for reasons that are only beginning to become apparent to me. And in his boundless grace, he's not only using cancer to bless me but to bless those around me.

Will I have cancer again? Possibly. Even if I do, though, cancer won't have the power to conquer my spirit. For I know that even if cancer so ravages my body that I no longer have the strength to go on living, I'll still win the battle. As Philippians 1:18, 21 so beautifully says: "I will continue to rejoice ... for to me, to live is Christ and to die is gain."[11]

CHAPTER TWO   GROWING IN GOD

power in short prayers

God listens to my prayers wherever I am. That didn't sink in until my son, Chris, left to attend a university twenty hours from home. Oh, how I missed hearing his voice.

Busy with pre-med classes, intramural basketball, and studying, Chris didn't call often. But once in a while, the phone would ring, and it would be Chris. I'd drop everything—the project I was working on, dinner preparations—just to hear my son's voice.

One day I realized God felt the same way about me, only hundreds of times more, because I'm his child (John 1:12). Whether I'm walking, driving across town, or sending a prayer heavenward from my computer, he delights in hearing from me, not just once a day, but throughout the day. As Psalms 40:1 and 34:15 say, God turns to me and his ears are attentive to my prayers.

I became even more excited about the effects of praying continuously when I noticed that throughout the Bible, God used short prayers to accomplish great things, such as raising the dead or parting the Red Sea. It dawned on me that though it's wonderful to have extended sessions of prayer, short prayers can also have a big impact. That encourages me to pray throughout the day.[1]

Postures of Prayer

One look at my packed Day-Timer and you'd think I single-handedly feel responsible to bring in God's kingdom. I try hard to make a difference in my community and the world, yet despite all the mothering, befriending, organizing, volunteering, and ministering, it's easy for me to feel helpless before the onslaught of our culture's decay.

When I feel overwhelmed by a feeling of powerlessness, I need to remember one of the most potent defenses I have against it. Prayer puts me in touch with the God who is in charge of everything and who promises to be faithful.

Consider the classic postures of prayer: hands folded and head bowed, arms raised with palms to the sky, kneeling or lying on the ground with arms outstretched. All that speaks of utter helplessness to do anything and total abandonment to the Lord. Isn't it curious that the empty hands we bring to prayer are actually what strengthens our grip on hope?[2]

The Blessings of Cancer

When people ask why God would allow me to have breast cancer twice, I often say, "Why would he give me health? One is no more deserved than another."

I go on to tell them how God has used cancer for good in my life. For one thing, it's brought the reconciliation of my son and daughter. Sibling rivalry ruled these kids through childhood, teenage years, and well after both left home. But the day we learned the spot on my hip might be metastasized breast cancer, my son and daughter reached out for each other. As I watched them embrace, tears ran down my cheeks. If this is what cancer could accomplish, I was willing to have it.

There have been other blessings, too, such as priceless memories of my post-operative care. I think of how my daughter bathed me and washed my hair in the hospital. How my mother fixed tea and fetched me pillows, how my sisters dropped off meals, how my step-dad stocked the birdfeeder to entice the finches I love to watch. How friends kidnapped me for lunch. And, finally, how my husband helped me into the car for the long ride home. All the while, I was buoyed by people who were praying for me at work, at church, and in various support groups.

But the sweetest blessing is how cancer makes me cling to God. Life can be so busy that it may take something such as cancer to teach us that regardless of how rewarding our job, family, friendships, and church responsibilities are, nothing is more precious than the time we spend with God.[3]

GROWING IN GOD 17

PRAYER CONNECTION

Carole worked at home in Texas; I worked in an office in Illinois eleven hundred miles away. We mailed each other a list of our prayer concerns every week. At 10:00 a.m. every Tuesday morning, I dialed her phone number and let it ring once to signal I was available to pray. Then we each took a fifteen-minute break in a private place.

Separately, we joined together before God's throne. Each Tuesday morning the miles between us disappeared as we prayed for our concerns at the same time. Though we weren't together in person, Jesus kept his promise to be present when two or three gather in his name (Matt. 18:20).

With Carole, I've shared the joy of many answered prayers. We've seen needs met, rough places smoothed, relationships healed, circumstances changed, and faith strengthened. When the answers came, my prayer partner was the first to know. In the meantime, the load became lighter and the waiting easier.[4]

Even a vacation can be a time for spiritual renewal. **traveling with Jesus** ////

Some people say traveling or commuting offers great opportunities for communicating with Christ.

"Music is my key to keeping a relationship with God," says Denise, a drapery factory manager. "Since I travel quite a bit, I listen to Christian tapes or tune into a Christian radio station while I'm in the car. It's a great opportunity to sing along and praise God."

Women whose jobs require travel often find themselves in hotel rooms with no concrete plans after the workday ends. They can use that time well by dedicating it to Christ.

Even a vacation can be a time for spiritual renewal. Ask your husband to take the kids to the hotel pool while you spend a few uninterrupted moments studying your Bible.

If you spend a lot of time waiting in school parking lots, airports, train stations, or doctor's offices, you can turn wasted minutes into times of spiritual growth.

"God has a heart for busy people," says Sandy, a cheerleading coach, school aide, and mother of four, who spends much of her time in her van. "But my Bible is in the car, and when I'm waiting to pick up one of my kids, I open it."

The supreme guide for the Christian life is, of course, the Bible. Bibles are available in many versions and sizes, often at a low cost. So put a copy of God's Word in your desk, car, briefcase, backpack, purse, locker, diaper bag, or bathroom magazine rack.

Devotional helps are available in wonderful variety in bookstores. Even secular bookstores may have helpful guides for you to tuck into your Bible for further study.

But neither Bible nor devotional books will help us if we're surprised by thirty beautifully-free minutes and the study materials are nowhere to be found. "I make sure I keep my Bible and study book in the same place in my den so I can find them easily," says Marianne, a professor. "If I have to spend even five minutes looking for a pen, there goes part of my study time."[5]

JUMP-START YOUR QUIET TIME

Enough with the excuses. Here are ten ways to revitalize your time with God:

1. Begin a prayer journal. A simple spiral notebook will do. Keep track of your prayer requests and praises. Better yet, write out your prayers to God.

2. Study Psalm 119 for a month. Read six verses each day and write down the blessings and benefits of knowing God's Word.

3. Ask a friend to be your study buddy. Study the same book of the Bible and meet regularly to discuss what God is teaching you.

4. Make a list of everything you're thankful for, from sunshine to God's gift of salvation. Refer to this list often, especially when you're frustrated or discouraged.

5. Pray Scripture for yourself, your family, or friends. For example, for salvation, read: Isaiah 45:3, 2 Timothy 2:10; for purity: Psalm 51:10; for joy: 1 Thessalonians 1:6; for love of God's Word: Psalm 19:9–10.

6. Incorporate Christian music into your quiet time. Read or sing the words of a favorite hymn or listen to a praise CD. Contemplate how the lyrics draw you closer to God.

7. Read your favorite psalm, then write your own paraphrase of it, personalizing the Psalm to fit your circumstances.

8. Vary your setting. If you normally have your quiet time indoors, try praying while you walk through the woods, or bring your Bible and meditate by a quiet stream.

9. Establish a family quiet time. Read a Bible passage together and discuss it. Share prayer requests and take turns praying for one another. Encourage your children to act out one of their favorite Bible stories, complete with costumes and props.

10. Listen to God. Ask him to free you from distractions, then sit quietly and allow him to speak to you.[6]

All over the world this gospel is bearing fruit and growing, just as it has been doing among you since the day you heard it and understood God's grace in all its truth. —Colossians 1:6

hope in loss

MY NEIGHBOR JOHN LEARNED ABOUT TRUE HOPE WHEN HE WAS A YOUNG BOY IN THE NETHERLANDS. HIS MOTHER LAY DYING IN THE HOUSE. JOHN RAN TO THE BARN WHERE HE WAITED IN FEAR THAT SOMEONE WOULD COME TO TELL HIM WHAT HE MOST DREADED TO HEAR. WHEN THE FOOTSTEPS CAME, THEY WERE THOSE OF HIS FATHER, SHUFFLING AND HEAVY.

John recounted his father's words with tears. "John, your mother is gone. Now we must sing praise to God." And so the brokenhearted young husband and his little boy began to sing Psalm 42.

Young John was taught by a wise, yet grieving, father to sneak a look at the last page. He was learning to see beyond earthly things to a hope that's based on a faithful God who keeps his promises. He was being taught to focus "not on what is seen, but on what is unseen, [since] what is seen is temporary, but what is unseen is eternal" (2 Cor. 4:18).

That's how it is with true hope. We can live in absolute certainty that, no matter what our circumstances are, God is in control. We are hooked into the very character of God with the anchor of Christ. Regardless of our ability to keep our grip, the Lord keeps his grip on us.

As Hebrews 6:19-20 says, "We have this hope as an anchor for the soul, firm and secure. It enters the inner sanctuary behind the curtain, where [our forerunner] Jesus ... has entered on our behalf."[7]

GROWING IN GOD 21

4 ways to tell
if a church
really cares

When people in the seats around you introduce themselves before or after the services.

When the pastor or a visitation team offers to visit you in your home.

When people your age or in your stage of life invite you to participate in events.

When the church meets special needs through divorce- and grief-recovery groups, or other opportunities to integrate newcomers into community.

A CARING CHURCH

my friend Gail is single and age forty. She moved cross-country three years ago because of a job transfer. Gail looks to church as her main source of friendship and nurture. She says she loves the church she found when she relocated. "People show they care about me by asking me to get involved in projects," she says.

My family and I tried a new church just a few weeks before my mom and I arrived at the hospital emergency room at 5:00 a.m. to see my dad rolling into cardiac surgery. We held his hands for a moment, then let go as he made the solitary journey toward the operation that would either save his life or end it.

We prayed. We watched the second hand of the waiting-room clock make its methodical sweep. We barely spoke.

Finally, at 12:50 p.m., a stone-faced waiting-room attendant ushered us into a private room to await the surgeon's report. My mother and I stared at the vacant hall until a glowing face peered around the corner. It was Ted Olsen, a pastor from the church we'd been visiting. He squeezed our hands and prayed with us as we awaited word about Dad. We knew that a church whose pastor genuinely cared for newcomers as much as for its faithful members was a strong contender in our search for a church home.[8]

WE CONTINUALLY ASK GOD TO FILL YOU WITH THE KNOWLEDGE OF HIS WILL THROUGH ALL THE WISDOM AND UNDERSTANDING THAT THE SPIRIT GIVES, SO THAT YOU MAY LIVE A LIFE WORTHY OF THE LORD AND PLEASE HIM IN EVERY WAY: BEARING FRUIT IN ALL GOOD WORK, GROWING IN THE KNOWLEDGE OF GOD. —COLOSSIANS 1:9–10 TNIV

MENTORING DONNA

GOD GAVE ME THE COURAGE TO ASK DONNA IF I COULD BE HER MENTOR AND HER LIFE WAS TRANSFORMED

Several years ago, I became friends with a fellow school bus driver named Donna. She and I spent a year of shared layovers talking about many topics, but our conversations usually returned to Donna's anxiety about the turmoil in her home. She often commented about my peaceful attitude no matter what my circumstances.

I treasured those opportunities and spoke openly about the difference Christ has made in my life. At God's nudging, I made a bookmark for Donna with Isaiah 26:3 TNIV on it: "You will keep in perfect peace those whose minds are steadfast, because they trust in you."

I was thrilled when Donna began attending my church. When I prayed for other ways to help my friend learn about Jesus, God gave me the courage to ask Donna if I could be her mentor. Donna readily accepted my offer, and we began meeting to read the Bible together and discuss faith issues. After a short time, Donna asked Jesus to be her Savior. Her life was transformed. Donna is now growing strong in her faith, and her family members even accompany her to church on occasion.

But God wasn't finished. My relationship with Donna inspired me to start a women's mentoring ministry at our church. Many women have been blessed through that ministry. Just think, it all started because of God's nudging me to share my faith at work.[9]

CHAPTER THREE REST

a good sabbath

There's an old Puritan saying: "Good Sabbaths make good Christians." Honoring the Sabbath was easier in Puritan New England, where almost everyone took the Sabbath seriously.

Shops weren't open on Sundays, businesses closed their doors, and everyone headed to church. Sabbaths are much more difficult today. In a society that values busyness and productivity, observing the Sabbath is downright countercultural.

That's not to say our society doesn't encourage us to relax. To the contrary, most secular women's magazines and television talk shows (not to mention Calgon ads) urge us to de-stress. While there's nothing wrong with an occasional bubble bath, Calgon days aren't quite the same thing as Sabbath rest. The key to the Sabbath isn't merely rest; rather, it's that in our rest we turn our attention to God, whom we mirror in our rest.

So how, in our hectic world, can we set apart a day truly given to rest and reverence?

I've found it helpful to mark the beginning of the Sabbath by gathering on Saturday night with friends for an unhurried time of food, fellowship, and prayer.

I also keep in mind the two commandments that govern Jewish Sabbath observance: to not work on the Sabbath and to be joyful. So on Sundays, I don't shop, I don't grade papers, and I don't touch my phone. I try not to start planning for the week ahead. Instead, I do things that will give me spiritual joy. I take long walks with friends. I allow extra time for Bible study.

Christian Sabbath observance isn't so much about rules as orientation. It's taking a break from the busyness of the week and turning towards the Creator who also rested from his labor. In this rest we find a true sense of Shabbat shalom, Sabbath peace.[1]

COME TO ME, ALL YOU WHO ARE WEARY AND BURDENED, AND I WILL GIVE YOU REST. TAKE MY YOKE UPON YOU AND LEARN FROM ME, FOR I AM GENTLE AND HUMBLE IN HEART, AND YOU WILL FIND REST FOR YOUR SOULS. —MATTHEW 11:28–29

Enjoying Sunday

Sundays used to make me angry. As a young girl, I found the afternoons after church stretched out interminably while my parents rested, talked, or listened to Billy Graham on the radio.

How can they stand it? I thought, restlessly. *This is so-o-o boring.* My friends couldn't come by on Sunday, and all work came to a standstill (except for my mom's cooking of Sunday dinner).

What was lost on me as a child is how remarkable God's gift of rest is to us, his weary children. Like stubborn two-year-olds who fight naptime with pouting lips and stomping feet, we resist the very thing that's good for us, the very thing we so desperately need.

"Stop what you're doing," God commands us. "Worship me and rest. Catch a fresh vision of what life in my kingdom is like. Enjoy my good gifts. Rest."

Perhaps grudgingly we put down our important projects along with our certainty that we're in control. With a long glance backward, we leave the lists and the calendars and join with other pouting children who gather to rest in the Father's love. Standing shoulder to shoulder in worship, we push aside the work project deadlines or the grief over a struggling marriage to sing, "Great is Thy faithfulness. Morning by morning new mercies I see." The hymn reminds us of the hope that comes when God's people proclaim his Lordship over all schedules, all circumstances, all struggles.

Leaning into the songs of faith, we are encouraged to rest, to fellowship, to enjoy God's gifts of food and laughter. Curiously, we find that in quietness and confidence we find strength (Isa. 30:15). During this time we are given the resources to go on to another week.[2]

Sleep to Your Health

The first big step toward getting healthy is getting enough sleep. Keeping regular sleeping hours is crucial because other health builders, such as eating right and exercising, are harder to implement if you're exhausted.

The problem is, prior to bedtime many of us get involved in a book or movie or some work project, such as cleaning the kitchen. Those things distract the body from preparing for sleep. Look at what you're doing late in the day, and make wiser choices to help your body and mind wind down so you can sleep.

One of the best things you can do is turn off the television and computer at least an hour before bedtime. Artificial light from the computer or television stimulates your nervous system, making it harder for you to fall asleep.

Our culture expects us to run ourselves ragged on an inhuman schedule. Don't buy into this. Lots of truly exhausted people have trouble falling asleep because their minds are still racing. Maybe they've worked hard mentally but haven't exerted their body all day. That makes it tough to get a good night's sleep.

If this is your problem, try taking a bath. Turn down the phone ringer. Turn down the bright lights and lower the sound. Unwind for an hour, then go to bed.

The payoff comes the next morning when you wake up well rested and ready to celebrate a new, God-given day.[3]

My soul finds rest IN GOD ALONE; MY SALVATION COMES FROM HIM. HE ALONE IS MY ROCK AND MY SALVATION; HE IS MY FORTRESS, I WILL NEVER BE SHAKEN. —PSALM 62:1–2

GETTING ENOUGH SLEEP

You need seven to nine hours of sleep per night according to the National Sleep Foundation. Not getting enough sleep has been linked to health problems such as obesity, high blood pressure, negative mood and behavior, and decreased productivity. Here are a few tips from the foundation to help you establish and maintain good sleep habits:

1. **Go to bed** and get up about the same time every day.

2. **Establish** a regular, relaxing bedtime routine, such as soaking in a hot bath or listening to soothing music.

3. **Keep** work materials, computer, and television out of the sleeping environment.

4. **Finish** eating at least two to three hours before your regular bedtime.

5. **Exercise** regularly, but complete your workout at least three hours before your bedtime.[4]

SLEEP PROBLEMS IN MARRIAGE

If you want to be intimate with your spouse, but you can't seem to sleep together without losing much-needed sleep, here are some strategies to help:

1. Buy the right bed. If your bed squeaks every time somebody rolls over or is so narrow that your spouse knocks you every time he moves, a simple solution may be to buy a new, larger bed.

2. Reduce noise. For many couples, the main sleep problem they face is noise, whether from snoring or periodic interruptions, such as phone calls. You can take steps to reduce snoring, but if you're plagued by noises of other sorts, consider earplugs.

3. Sleep apart. If none of these solutions works, you may have to consider sleeping apart. Many of us balk at this idea because we're scared of sacrificing the intimacy of sharing a bed. But if you put your mind to it, you can preserve intimacy and still protect your sleep.

If you're going to sleep apart, try going to bed together a little earlier than you usually go to sleep. Take that time to share a psalm, talk about your day, and share what's on your mind. After you've spent time together, separate before actually going to sleep.

To avoid any resentment, take turns being the one to leave the bed so that both spouses get to enjoy the bedroom. Be sure to tell your children (and others who need to know) about the sleeping arrangements, so they won't assume your marriage is on the rocks.

Finally, make sure you're both okay with the sleeping arrangement. Remember, the problem takes two: he may thrash or snore, but you're easily awakened by any noise. It's not time to lay blame; it's just time to get some sleep.[5]

GIVE STRESS A REST

Jesus reminded us in Matthew 6:34 to live in the present, essentially relaxing, because, "Each day has enough trouble of its own." You may be really stressed out right now. But soon that situation will pass and, chances are, you'll soon be in a calmer, more relaxed time.

Stress becomes more manageable if it doesn't carry with it the weight of past problems, such as: "My boss always waits until the last minute to do these mailings" or "My team leader never asks my opinion." Such "kitchen sink" thinking—piling onto a problem everything but the kitchen sink—sabotages solutions by sheer poundage.

Besides, when has piling more weight on problems really solved anything? We live in a fallen world. But instead of stressing out over your problems, give your mind a rest by asking, "How much of this will matter in five, ten, or one hundred years?"

In the midst of the ups and downs of life, remember: If our lives are anchored in Christ, the Prince of Peace, and we're standing upon the Solid Rock, then we can survive, even thrive, as we rest in him.[6]

He gives strength TO THE WEARY AND INCREASES THE POWER OF THE WEAK. EVEN YOUTHS GROW TIRED AND WEARY, AND YOUNG MEN STUMBLE AND FALL; BUT THOSE WHO HOPE IN THE LORD WILL RENEW THEIR STRENGTH. THEY WILL SOAR ON WINGS LIKE EAGLES; THEY WILL RUN AND NOT GROW WEARY, THEY WILL WALK AND NOT BE FAINT. —ISAIAH 40:29–31

FIGHTING WORKAHOLISM

There is no quick fix for workaholics; work habits are too ingrained. But the situation isn't hopeless.

If we who gravitate toward idolatrous overwork turn to Christ, we can begin to rest, knowing that the God who created us and cares for us will free us from overworking, carry us when we are tired, and give us power to live to God's glory. As Jesus promises in Matthew 11:28: "Come to me, all you who are weary and burdened, and I will give you rest."

As Christians fighting this battle, we have other weapons available to us. Some of them are:

1. Making God our first priority. God calls us to put him first in our lives. We seek his kingdom first by spending time with God through the study of Scripture and prayer. That helps us tune into the still, small voice of God to gain his perspective on the daily choices we make in our lives.

2. Getting some Christian counseling. Working with a therapist can be particularly effective in healing deeper issues contributing to workaholism.

3. Taking the Sabbath seriously. Setting aside one day each week to rest and worship God gives us a much-needed break from work and its burdens.

4. Leaning on Christ. Jesus understands our problems with overwork and exhaustion. And he is infinitely more powerful than workaholism. Rest in his power, not yours, to relieve you from work addiction.[7]

unplugging entertainment

THE WEEK BEFORE MY FAMILY UNPLUGGED ITSELF FROM ALL FORMS OF HIGH-TECH ENTERTAINMENT AS RESEARCH FOR AN ARTICLE I WAS WRITING, WE GLUTTED OURSELVES ON ELECTRONIC STIMULI, PLAYING COMPUTER GAMES FOR HOURS AND WATCHING RERUNS OF ALL OUR FAVORITE TV SHOWS.

When our media-fast week arrived, I was amazed at how much more time we had as individuals and as a family. How did we fill that time? Games and puzzles came in handy. One of our favorites was Hot Potato. Whoever was holding the potato when it burped was out of the game. (Finding this so entertaining is either a testament to our creative abilities or proof that we need to get out of the house more often.)

More rewarding was watching my girls interact in creative play. They schemed. They brainstormed. They ransacked my office for scissors, cardboard, markers, and tape. They debated, reconciled, negotiated, bartered, and giggled.

As the week drew to a close, everyone chattered happily about being reunited with his or her favorite media addiction. My husband, Larry, was eager to re-claim Planet Earth from alien forces, Kaitlyn missed sending electronic greeting cards to her friends, and Kacie was simply relieved to know the TV was going to mysteriously start working again at midnight on Sunday.

At 10:45 p.m. Sunday, Larry and I assessed our media-free week. In the past, we had tried to create quality family time by adding more things to our already busy schedule. Now we suspected the best way to bond as a family was to take things out.[8]

THE LORD IS MY SHEPHERD, I SHALL NOT BE IN WANT. HE MAKES ME LIE DOWN IN GREEN PASTURES, HE LEADS ME BESIDE QUIET WATERS, HE RESTORES MY SOUL. HE GUIDES ME IN PATHS OF RIGHTEOUSNESS FOR HIS NAME'S SAKE. —PSALM 23:1–3

practicing peace

My husband and I had just returned home from a hectic shopping trip. Erik pulled into the driveway and switched off the engine. We were suddenly surrounded by the silence of the night. We sat in the darkness; reluctant to give up the first quiet moment we'd experienced that entire day. I sighed, tired from the day's activities and the thoughts of the coming day's responsibilities.

Worn down by busyness and worries, I longed to be enveloped in the peace of God, that deep serenity of soul where calm and joy grow. But I had to admit that in the many years I'd been a Christian I hadn't experienced much peace. Was the peace the Bible spoke of just some distant theological doctrine, or was it something I could actually experience now?

Several days later, I read Philippians 4:6–7 and was surprised that this passage that speaks of the peace of God also states clearly how to obtain it: "Do not be anxious about anything, but in everything, by prayer and petition, with thanksgiving, present your requests to God. And the peace of God, which transcends all understanding, will guard your hearts and your minds in Christ Jesus." While I was familiar with those concepts, I had to admit that I wasn't actually practicing them. But my heart longed for peace, so I decided to test this biblical recipe to see what would happen.

Some time after taking on the challenge of Philippians 4, I was on my way to help a friend move when it suddenly struck me what a difference this Scripture passage had made in my life. I was still busy. I still had family, work, and church responsibilities. But somehow life was different. I was different. While the change happened subtly over time, I know now how it feels to be enveloped in God's peace. And I thank him for it.[9]

DO NOT BE ANXIOUS ABOUT ANYTHING, BUT IN EVERYTHING, BY PRAYER AND PETITION, WITH THANKSGIVING, PRESENT YOUR REQUESTS TO GOD. AND THE PEACE OF GOD, WHICH TRANSCENDS ALL UNDERSTANDING, WILL GUARD YOUR HEARTS AND YOUR MINDS IN CHRIST JESUS. —PHILIPPIANS 4:6-7

BACKYARD VACATION

One of the wonders of going on a vacation is taking a break from the daily grind. You can enjoy the beauty God has created, take in wonderful fragrances of the outdoors, eat delicious foods, relax, and unwind. But by the time you do everything you need to do to leave town, you're exhausted. And when you return, you're broke. Here are some great ways to escape and relax in your own backyard:

1. Relax to nature's sounds. Place a bird feeder or birdhouse in your backyard and fill it with sunflower seeds, a favorite of birds. Birds also love bushes with berries and nectar-filled flowers. As the birds discover your friendly fare, your home will become a favorite place for them, and their singing will make your backyard a sanctuary.

Wind chimes will also help you relax as they gently make music with the whispering of the wind.

2. Add your own music. Certain moments call for simply staring at the stars and listening to crickets chirping on a clear night. But if you want to feel like you're in the Bahamas, try basking in the sun while listening to Jimmy Buffett. Throw a Frisbee to the singing of The Beach Boys, or dine to beautiful instrumentals.

3. Let water soothe you. You can enjoy the gentle sound of trickling water from a small, flowing fountain as it turns your garden or patio into a soothing oasis. Many attractive fountains are relatively inexpensive and contain pumps that recirculate the water, so no plumbing is needed.

4. Swing a little. Swinging or rocking makes life seem carefree. For an afternoon siesta, cozy up in a hammock in a shady spot in your backyard. Hang a swinging bench on your porch or treat yourself to a rocker built for two.[10]

- create a backyard nature sanctuary
- gaze at the stars and listen to the crickets
- add a water attraction
- enjoy delicious foods

CHAPTER FOUR   ENTERTAINMENT

taking your dream trip
If you think you'll never be able to afford your dream trip, think again. Here are some ways to make it happen:

1. Identify your destination. Do you dream of taking a whirlwind tour of Europe's most beautiful cities? A slow meander through Yosemite's National Park in autumn? An adventure package in Africa with a guide to lead the way? Name your heart's desire.

2. Make it visual. Get a map, travel posters, and photographs of this dream destination and hang them where you'll see them daily. Use them as your computer's screen saver. Research your destination and read novels set in that part of the world. Envision yourself in that dream location. What are you wearing? What are you doing? Where are you eating?

3. Calculate the cost. Add up the cost of transportation, lodging, meals, attractions, must sees, and must dos. Put money you ordinarily would spend on movies or dinner into a special travel account. Add to this other unexpected windfalls.

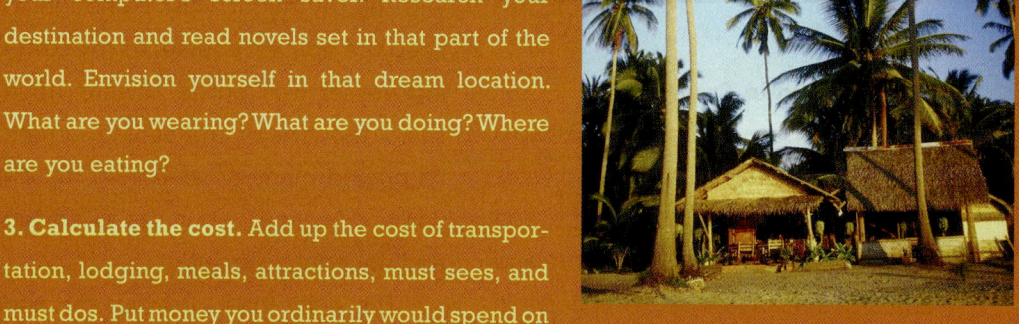

4. List necessities. Think through what you'll need for the climate, recreation, and culture of your destination. What clothing will you bring? Will you need protection from sun or rain? Sporting gear? Gifts for locals you may meet? A sleeping bag or travel mug?

5. Think of ways to reduce expenses. Could you do picnics instead of restaurants while at your destination? Might you stay in hostels instead of hotels? Walk instead of take the subway? Look on the Web for economical airfares, museum packages, or coupons for attractions.

6. Put it on the calendar. Put your projected date of departure on your calendar, though it may be years away. It's no longer just a dream; you're making it a reality![1]

Finding God in Travel

As a young believer, I took my first solo trip right after college. I spent two years working my way across Europe and the Middle East. I worked for room and board in a home for cast-off people in England, a bed-and-breakfast in Austria, a peanut farm in Israel, and a Jesus People barn in Bavaria. By the time I returned home, I had smuggled Bibles behind the Iron Curtain, been pelted with stones by boys in Gaza, endured endless nights sleeping on cold trains, and swam with a shark in the Red Sea.

I learned I was more resourceful than I knew. But most importantly, I found God in the most unlikely moments. I've learned to watch for his wonderful surprises in my life ever since.

Even now, as a mother of three adult daughters and living on a budget, I find travel a pivotal influence in my spiritual development. Not long ago, I camped with a group in the Pacific Northwest. While kayaking, I discovered that pulling on the oars with all my might wasn't enough to keep the boat on course. As my straying vessel was pulled toward open sea, I thought of the aching lament I'd prayed many times during my divorce: "Oh Lord, your sea is so big and my boat so small."

The guide had to rescue me and tow me back to shore. Coming face-to-face with my vulnerability that day taught me compassion for others adrift in shame or loss. The emotional impact of that traveling experience motivated me to train as a life coach to help guide people through the crosscurrents of their lives.[2]

HE WILL YET FILL YOUR MOUTH WITH LAUGHTER AND YOUR LIPS WITH SHOUTS OF JOY. —JOB 8:21

KEEPING LIFE AN ADVENTURE

You're never too old to travel.

In my fifties, I learned to snowboard with a class of college kids. Later my daughter and I backpacked through Europe. A friend treated herself to a kayak trip through Alaskan waterways to celebrate her big fiftieth. Another friend spent a weekend at a Christian hostel for women in New York City. She met plenty of New Yorkers as she helped serve meals at a rescue mission. Elderhostels are remarkable places to meet interesting people and see the world, too. I once met a sixty-something gentleman who'd been all the way to Timbuktu just to say he had.

Once you make that first step into unfamiliar terrain, you become God's apprentice in the holy art of living. Does that mean everything will go smoothly? That you'll come home with armloads of stunning photos? That you'll find fantastic souvenirs? Not necessarily. A journey is a metaphor for life. And life can get messy. But it can also give you fantastic spiritual insights.[3]

A JOURNEY IS A METAPHOR FOR LIFE. AND LIFE CAN GET MESSY. BUT IT CAN ALSO GIVE YOU FANTASTIC SPIRITUAL INSIGHTS.

ENTERTAINMENT 37

FINALLY, BROTHERS, WHATEVER IS TRUE, WHATEVER IS NOBLE, WHATEVER IS RIGHT, WHATEVER IS PURE, WHATEVER IS LOVELY, WHATEVER IS ADMIRABLE — IF ANYTHING IS EXCELLENT OR PRAISEWORTHY — THINK ABOUT SUCH THINGS. —PHILIPPIANS 4:8

praying through the news

I love the news. Like coffee, I want my news unadorned, straightforward, and hot. So I begin my day with the local morning show, catch the national evening news, then top off the day with late-night news. I read a daily newspaper and two weekly local papers as well as the Sunday edition. My Internet homepage is programmed to report world and national news headlines, and my car radio is tuned to my favorite news station.

Recently, though, my media consumption became a concern. I began suffering from higher levels of anxiety, headaches, and insomnia. After a thorough exam to rule out physical causes, my physician suggested my devotion to world events was taking its toll. It was literally making me sick. I realized I was paying more attention to the problems of the world than to the Problem Solver I served.

One day, I read an article on intercessory prayer that highlighted a prayer group that meets weekly. The members share newspaper clippings they collect through the week and pray for the people and events in the articles. Suddenly my avid interest in the news no longer seems like a medical condition, but a calling.

If you're a similarly afflicted newshound, consider that God may be calling you, too, to pray regularly for the world.[4]

tuning out tv marriage

IF YOU GET YOUR INFORMATION ABOUT RELATIONSHIPS FROM TV, YOU'RE GOING TO THINK THERE'S SOMETHING INADEQUATE ABOUT YOURS

Television can be harmful to marriage.

A few years ago, The National Fatherhood Initiative announced that "few fathers are to be found on prime-time television, and those that are usually are portrayed as incompetent or detached." The typical TV father resembles Homer Simpson, a jolly buffoon who may mean well but who constantly requires his wife and kids to bail him out of scrapes. Other shows highlight a husband's inadequacies by going to the opposite extreme: men on soap operas constantly bring flowers and chocolates to their beloved wives while hanging onto their every word. Women who watch such shows may expect too little or too much from their husbands.

Television's depiction of mothers can be equally as harmful. Women on television rarely concern themselves with mundane things, such as cleaning, laundry, or errands. Instead, TV mothers are energetic and competent, juggling everything without getting a hair out of place. None of this tires them out, either; at night they're eager for sex, regardless of problems with the kids. Men watching such shows find their own wives inexplicably unaffectionate and petty in comparison.

These unrealistic images worry Denise MacDonald, a marriage and family therapist from Ontario. "If you get your information about relationships from TV, you're going to think there's something inadequate about yours," she says. Since such subjects are rarely discussed honestly among friends, the only window many of us have into how others handle relationship and sexual issues is TV. It's a great disappointment, then, when our spouses don't live up to this elusive "norm."

Reducing TV time is one way to combat these unwholesome images. We might be pleasantly surprised by what we'd find if we switched off, looked around us, and started enjoying our spouses and families again.[5]

RENEWAL IS ONLY ONE BENEFIT OF A VACATION. TIME AWAY FROM HOME PROMISES REFRESHMENT, BUT IT ALSO GUARANTEES CHANGE. YOU'LL COME BACK AS A SLIGHTLY DIFFERENT PERSON BECAUSE OF THE SIGHTS YOU'VE SEEN, THE PEOPLE YOU'VE MET, THE CONVERSATIONS YOU'VE HAD, THE IDEAS YOU'VE ABSORBED.

HOMECOMING AFTER VACATION

You so looked forward to that stay at the beach or that weekend business conference mixed with sightseeing. What you didn't look forward to was coming home to the blinking red eye of your answering machine, the pile of mail, the empty fridge, and the oh-so-familiar feeling of letdown.

Stress-management counselor Julie Lee offers some tips to help you offset the funk that often follows the fun. Put these into practice, and you'll find the reentry from a getaway much easier.

1. Plan for your return. Clear your desk the best you can before going on vacation, and create a list of projects to tackle when you return. This gives you direction and answers the question, "What should I do first?" as you play catch-up at home or at the office. Schedule something fun on that to-do list so you'll have something to look forward to during the post-vacation blahs.

2. Stock the fridge. Fill the fridge with the ingredients for two days' worth of meals so you won't have to dash to the grocery store after you get back from vacation. Buy a book you've been eager to read and leave it on your nightstand as a welcome-home gift. Put fresh towels and bubble bath by the tub.

3. Make a list. As your holiday winds down, use your time on the plane or in the car to list those aspects of home you most love and appreciate. If you're traveling with children, this can lead to interesting conversation. Concentrate on the simple pleasures you've missed while you've been away: working in your garden, having coffee with a friend, teaching Sunday school, babysitting for a neighbor's toddler. By reminding yourself of these pleasurable activities, you'll heighten your anticipation of homecoming.

4. Rest. Arrange to return from your vacation on Friday so you have the weekend to recover and regroup.

5. Put things into perspective. Renewal is only one benefit of a vacation. Time away from home promises refreshment, but it also guarantees change. You'll come back as a slightly different person because of the sights you've seen, the people you've met, the conversations you've had, and the ideas you've absorbed. Rather than mourning the end of a whirlwind experience, celebrate the new-and-improved you.[6]

CLEAR YOUR DESK THE BEST YOU CAN BEFORE GOING ON VACATION, AND CREATE A LIST OF PROJECTS TO TACKLE WHEN YOU RETURN. THIS GIVES YOU DIRECTION AND ANSWERS THE QUESTION, "WHAT SHOULD I DO FIRST?" AS YOU PLAY CATCH-UP AT HOME OR AT THE OFFICE.

ENTERTAINMENT 41

As your holiday winds down, USE YOUR TIME ON THE PLANE OR IN THE CAR TO LIST THOSE ASPECTS OF HOME YOU MOST LOVE AND APPRECIATE.

support

trust

accept

We dare to act silly with each other because we trust and accept each other.

my best friends

Cherry, Sue, Karen, Viki, Florence, and I met at church, where we all served in various ministries. About five years ago, Cherry and Sue started to meet over coffee to discuss problems they were having with their Sunday school kids. Karen joined them—then eventually so did Viki, Florence, and I. Though the kids outgrew their problems and we eventually resigned from our church duties, we discovered that we still wanted to get together.

To maintain contact, we have met regularly for coffee, where we've loved and supported each other through work problems, the deaths of parents, and personal injuries. Sometimes we trade recipes, books, and shopping tips. But when we gather once a year to celebrate our birthdays, the fun really begins.

Three years ago, when we were planning Sue's birthday, we searched for something fun to match her sense of humor. Someone suggested a Barbie theme in honor of Sue's hatred of Barbies. We all wore pink to the party and set the table with Barbie plates and napkins. Karen made a cake, with Barbie standing in the middle of a big skirt. We wore tiaras and waved magic wands. Once Sue got over her horror, she laughed and enjoyed the festivities.

While our coffees and conversations allow us to share problems and concerns, we set our everyday lives aside for our annual parties. They're purely for fun, a celebration of friendship. Our families support our parties, probably because we're all so happy preparing, attending, and remembering them.

We dare to act silly with each other because we trust and accept each other. As Pat says, "We know each other's foibles and share a common outlook. We know where we stand as sisters in Christ."[7]

FUN FOR TWO

OUR NEW TANDEM BICYCLE WOBBLED ACROSS THE ALLEY LIKE AN ERRANT BOWLING BALL. MY HUSBAND, STEVE, HIT THE BRAKES BEFORE WE HIT OUR NEIGHBOR'S TRASHCANS. HE RIPPED OFF HIS HELMET. "WEREN'T YOU READY?" "ALMOST." "I'LL BACK IT UP. THEN TELL ME WHEN YOU'RE READY!"

I glowered. For two cents, I'd have left him peddling alone. Unfortunately, our empty-nest present to each other cost more than two cents. So I forced myself back onto the bike.

Unlike Daisy and her suitor in the 1890s song, "Bicycle Built for Two," Steve and I have been together thirty years—sort of. Immersed in decades of work, 2:00 a.m. feedings, training bras, and teen drivers, we sometimes were so stressed we forgot each other's names. Now in middle age, we hoped our new bicycle would help us have fun together.

Instead, Steve and I found ourselves back in Marriage 101, relearning lessons we thought we'd mastered many years before.

Take body-image issues. My husband wears brown clothing one day, navy the next. But when he rides the bike, Steve dons eye-popping jerseys, a Star Wars-style helmet, and Spandex cycling shorts. In cold weather, he wears shiny red tights.

Discovering I was married to Captain America was one thing; sporting complimentary Catwoman attire was definitely another. "These shorts cut off my circulation!" I said, gawking at myself in the mirror. "I'd shame the kids!"

"The kids aren't here. We're doing this for us. Wear them." Steve grinned. "Besides, you look good."

The best part of this newfound recreation is that others do not suspect our true identities. During our snack break at a park shelter, a policeman, investigating reports of hanky-panky, prepared to order us out. Then he realized we were his parents' age.

"Sorry. Thought you were kids."

"We've been married thirty years." Innocence radiated from our wrinkles.

Perhaps the officer should not have left the scene.[8]

CHAPTER FIVE **HOME & HOSPITALITY**

helping homesick kids "Snow!" squealed a tiny voice from our living room. "Everyone, look, it's snow!" I recognized that voice with its lilting Jamaican accent. It belonged to a member of the college chorale group

to which my oldest daughter, Shelley, also belonged. The group had been on tour for several weeks. During their performance in our town, Shelley and several other singers were staying at our home.

I had often complained about Michigan's snow. But I had never before seen it through the eyes of an eager eighteen-year-old Jamaican girl. Melody's eyes turned to mine and I smiled. "Yes, the snow is beautiful, isn't it?"

The night before I had sipped a Coke with a young man who had told me about his parents' divorce. Shelley and another girl held his hands while he trembled and fought back tears.

These kids were eager for a home, not a hotel room. They had been too long on the road, were too far from home, and had had too much fast food and too many drives through the night. What these kids needed from us wasn't just a place to sleep. Rather, it was something that a friend, a Benedictine monk, described as, "Hospitality that makes room inside yourself for something else."

Scripture passages came to me that morning as I watched our house come alive with noise and activity: "Keep on loving one another as brothers and sisters. Do not forget to show hospitality to strangers" (Heb. 13:1–2 TNIV). "For I was hungry and you gave me something to eat, I was thirsty and you gave me something to drink, I was a stranger and you invited me in" (Matt. 25:35).[1]

ENTERTAINING STRANGERS

WHEN I FIRST PICKED UP CHRISTINE POHL'S MAKING ROOM, I THOUGHT I WOULD BE READING ABOUT INVITING PEOPLE OVER FOR DINNER OR MAKING SURE YOUR SON'S GIRLFRIEND FELT WELCOME WHEN SHE CAME TO VISIT.

But Pohl wrote the book because of her conviction that we must practice hospitality. Christians today are by and large inhospitable, Pohl says. "Hospitality is a nice extra if we have the time or resources, but we rarely view it as a spiritual obligation or as a dynamic expression of vibrant Christianity."

Pohl says that hospitality for Christians is "basic to who we are as followers of Jesus." It can be uncomfortable to show kindness to strangers, but Jesus did it, and so should we. Furthermore, the Bible requires the people of God to be hospitable. Hospitality is taught in Genesis 18, as Abraham and Sarah welcome three guests who prove to be angels. The passage is "unambiguously positive about welcoming strangers," Pohl says. "It connects hospitality with the presence of God, with promise, and with blessing."

In 1 and 2 Kings, Elisha and Elijah are both given shelter by women who barely know them. The guests then bring their hosts into special connection with God and give them other rewards as well. By contrast, consider what happens to people in the Old Testament who are inhospitable; the men of Sodom in Genesis 19 and Gibeah in Judges 19 are destroyed.

Pohl suggests that hospitality is integral to the overarching grand narrative of Israel's history. "Embedded within the covenant between God and Israel was Israel's identity as an alien and its related responsibility to sojourners and strangers," she says. The New Testament builds upon and transforms earlier teachings about hospitality. As Pohl says, "Jesus gave his life so that persons could be welcomed into the kingdom and in doing so linked hospitality, grace, and sacrifice in the deepest and most personal way imaginable."[2]

GIFT GIVING

The essence of giving is what motivates it. As Paul says in 2 Corinthians 9:7 TNIV: "Each of you should give what you have decided in your heart to give, not reluctantly or under compulsion, for God loves a cheerful giver." If your gift reflects duty or the expectation of reciprocity, it can't possibly convey cheerfulness. Other lessons about giving:

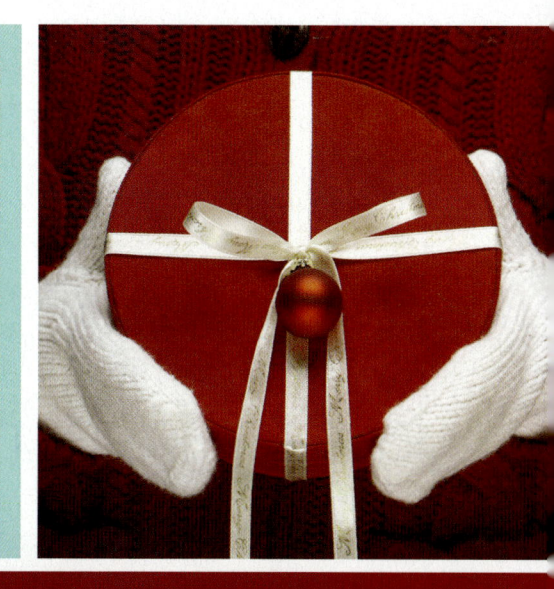

1. **A gift reflects the giver and its recipient.** My friend John shares my love of gardening. He raises hybrid daylilies as a hobby. A cardboard box of bare root daylilies shipped from his Michigan perennial beds to my California garden was an unforgettable gift. I unwrapped the damp newspaper surrounding the roots and tucked the roots into the soil near my window. Every summer when daylilies bloom, I think of John.

2. **A good gift affirms.** We provided our youngest daughter, who is an exceptional artist, with a drafting table for her room instead of the traditional desks we gave to the older two children. A desk would have worked just as well, but the drafting table stresses her individuality and says that we recognize her talent.

3. **The perfect gift isn't costly.** Luther Englund, a hospital chaplain, and his wife, Elvira, bake small loaves of bread and can homemade pomegranate jelly in baby food jars. Every year at Christmas, Luther takes a jar of jelly and a loaf of freshly baked bread to each man in a nearby prison. He knows this taste of home helps ease the loneliness of the holiday. The gift may be small, but the act of concern is priceless.

4. **A gift of memory is priceless.** My mother created a book of remembrances titled Bits 'N' Pieces for each person in our extended family. She compiled genealogical charts, recipes, family lore, photographs, and stories. It took her more than a year to complete these albums, and we'll savor the gift for a lifetime.

5. **Offer a gift that grows out of relationship.** Giving the perfect gift takes listening and planning. Sometimes it requires service and time. But long after gift-wrap and ribbons have been trashed, gifts of the heart remain.[3]

gardening for missions

WHEN PAT SCHILTZ'S DAUGHTER, MARLISE, NEEDED FINANCIAL SUPPORT TO DO MISSION WORK IN HONG KONG, PAT DECIDED TO HOST A COUNTRY GARDEN FAIRE ON THEIR FOUR-ACRE PROPERTY IN WAYNE, ILLINOIS.

Four hundred guests showed up to enjoy the breathtaking array of shell-pink poppies, blue larkspur, violet delphiniums, coral hollyhocks, and other flowers in her English country garden.

When Marlise signed up for another mission trip, Pat did a second garden tour. This time, attendance grew to twelve hundred. The extra money was given to other missionaries.

The next year, Marlise didn't go on a mission trip. But interest in Pat's garden fairs was so high that Pat agreed to host a two-day event. This time the focus was overtly evangelistic. Pat found numerous creative ways to plant seeds of faith during the fair. Throughout the garden, she placed signs with Scripture verses and poetry. She also recruited Christian friends to warmly greet visitors. Pat's husband, Jim, helped park cars. As guests arrived, they were handed a program containing Bible verses, a list of thirty-nine exhibitors of arts and handcrafts, and a welcome letter from Pat, saying, "The relaxation, joy, and peace we feel in a garden comes, I believe, because man was created in a garden. Whenever we wander into a garden or work in the soil, we are, in a very real sense, returning home.

"It is my earnest hope and prayer that while here you will personally draw closer to our Creator, the Master Gardener, and that you will grow in your knowledge of God's love for you."[4]

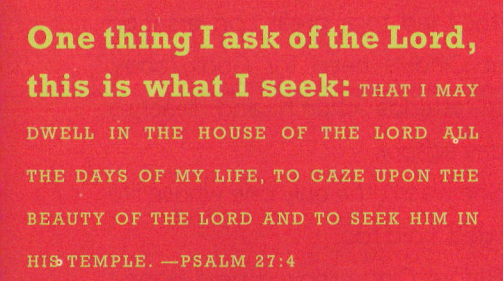

One thing I ask of the Lord, this is what I seek: THAT I MAY DWELL IN THE HOUSE OF THE LORD ALL THE DAYS OF MY LIFE, TO GAZE UPON THE BEAUTY OF THE LORD AND TO SEEK HIM IN HIS TEMPLE. —PSALM 27:4

WELCOMING NEW NEIGHBORS

OUR RELATIONSHIP WITH OUR NEW NEIGHBOR GOT OFF TO A ROCKY START WHEN CINDY'S SON NICK LET LOOSE WITH PROFANITY WHILE PLAYING BASKETBALL IN OUR BACKYARD. MY HUSBAND, MARK, LET NICK AND CINDY KNOW THAT KIND OF LANGUAGE WAS UNACCEPTABLE AT OUR HOUSE.

Cindy was embarrassed, but time passed, and eventually she asked me to recommend a church. I invited Cindy to our church but didn't tell her that Mark was the pastor.

As Cindy sat with me in the service, she looked puzzled as she looked at the man in the pulpit. Then she whispered, "I live next door to a preacher!" I knew God was at work when Cindy came back on her own the next Sunday.

Previously I would have marched right into Cindy's life with instructions on how she needed to forgive her ex-husband and get involved in the singles program at our church. Now I had a new approach: I kept my mouth shut, prayed, and waited for God to act.

One evening, Cindy came over with some self-help tapes she wanted me to listen to. They were pretty wild, but they led to a great conversation about Cindy's need for God. Today, Cindy attends church and teaches Sunday school.

She wasn't the only one whose life changed. I did too.

Before Cindy moved next door, I had kept my neighbors at a safe distance, talking to them in the yard or over the fence but rarely inviting them into our home. Yet I found that the best times I had with Cindy were over the impromptu meals we shared or our chats on the back porch while our kids played basketball. So now we learned to do that with other neighbors as well. Both Mark and I have been encouraged by the results.[5]

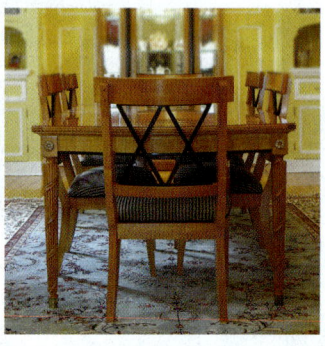

MAKING FRIENDS AROUND THE BLOCK

In *The Joy of Hospitality*, author Vonette Bright encourages life sharing.

That seems simple enough. But the book goes on to encourage us to invite people over, even when it feels uncomfortable. "You may be thinking, I could never do this in my neighborhood," Bright writes. "But it isn't the kind of people who live close to us that determines whether we minister or not; it's the great God whom we serve."

Since we began opening our home to others, we have found this to be true. We've seen God work through our hospitality, and that has far outweighed any hesitancy or fears about inviting people over. My attitude has also changed toward our neighbors. I stopped seeing them as targets for evangelism and began viewing them as people I needed to befriend.

BUT AS FOR ME AND MY HOUSEHOLD, WE WILL SERVE THE LORD. —JOSHUA 24:15

People who felt threatened by my former aggressiveness seemed to sense my new attitude. And they, in turn, ministered to me. For example, I was suffering from a terrible cold when my neighbor Jeanne called to see how I was feeling. I had a choice—to be honest and say, "I feel awful," or to be proud and say, "I'm fine."

I was honest, and when Jeanne brought over soup, I got tears in my eyes. Although Jeanne had earlier abandoned her Christian roots, she and I connected more through her act of kindness than from anything I had done for her. Our friendship helped her reconnect with her faith and with other Christians. Eventually God brought her husband, Pete, to faith in Christ as well.[6]

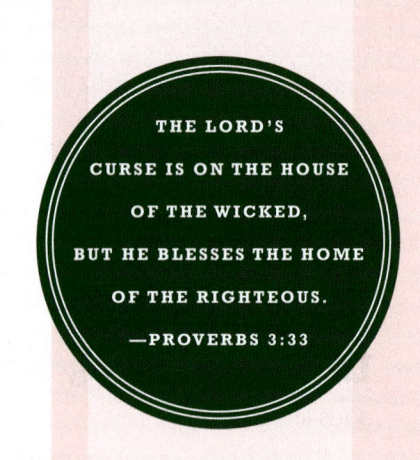

> THE LORD'S CURSE IS ON THE HOUSE OF THE WICKED, BUT HE BLESSES THE HOME OF THE RIGHTEOUS.
> —PROVERBS 3:33

FINDING GOD IN A MOBILE HOME

THE DAY WE MOVED INTO OUR TINY MOBILE HOME, ALL I NOTICED WERE CLUMPS OF MUD, STEADY DRIZZLE, OPPRESSIVE HEAT, AND MY CHILDREN'S DEJECTED LOOKS. AS MY THREE CHILDREN MOVED THEIR POSSESSIONS IN, THEY BARELY CONTAINED THEIR FRUSTRATION.

They didn't want to leave the middle-class home they were used to any more than I did. But with my twenty-two-year marriage ending in divorce, we had no choice.

I was also crying inside. Filled with self-pity, I was unable to rest in the Lord.

I gave my children bedroom rights as we moved in. Julie and Jennifer scrambled for the cramped front bedroom, leaving the other closet-sized bedroom to Jay. The living room became my bedroom. It would do, even though I had to watch the volume on my radio because of the paper-thin wall that separated the girls' bedroom from mine. But I didn't give up listening to my nightly program on Christian radio. The program provided me with peace during those first weeks of adjusting to our miniature quarters and an unfamiliar neighborhood.

Almost two years after moving into the mobile home, I turned on my radio to hear the familiar words and music. God's peace and comfort drifted over me as I listened to a clear call for people to respond to God's plan of salvation. The program ended. I began to drift off to sleep when I heard a muffled sound at the foot of my bed. My daughter, Julie, was quietly weeping. "Mom, I heard your radio program again tonight through the wall, and it seemed as though Jesus was talking just to me."

What joy! Despite my grumbling, God had used the move to this tiny house to carry his Word into my daughter's heart. The cramped, dreary quarters of our mobile home suddenly seemed beautiful as my daughter invited Jesus into her life.[7]

CLEANING OUT THE CLUTTER

In the big picture of life, dust balls don't matter. But taking time to clean the clutter out of our homes can actually clear away stress. Creating a home that is orderly and clean can bring a sense of calm and peace to our overloaded lives and our stressed-out marriages. So to freshen up your home, try these suggestions.

1. Have a plan. Write down on your calendar what tasks you want to do and when. Break the work into realistic pieces so it doesn't become overwhelming. Remember, God didn't create the world in one day; he did it one step at a time.

2. Celebrate your differences. In most marriages, one partner can get more done faster while the other gets less done but does an immaculate job. We need each other.

3. Define your domain. Before you criticize your mate for a messy desk, take a look at your workspace. If your area calls for improvement, start there. Actions speak louder than words, and the greatest inspiration is a good example.

4. Gather cleaning supplies. Load up a plastic bucket with cleaning supplies, paper towels, a scrub brush, and dust cloths, and carry it with you from room to room.

5. Make it fun. Playing upbeat music lifts your spirits and raises your energy. Also, offer yourself small rewards or incentives to keep going, such as going to a movie if you get the entire basement cleaned by 5:00 p.m.

6. Bag it. Take four large boxes or trash bags and label them: one for throw-aways, one for give-aways, one for store-aways, and one for keepers. As you move from room to room, take the stuff stashed in closets, corners, or drawers and put it in the appropriate box or bag. Then file back only the stuff worth saving.

Remember, the most important part of your home isn't your possessions, but the people under your roof. Keep kissing your mate while you're kissing your dirt and junk good-bye.[8]

A BEAUTIFUL BEDROOM

When you step into your bedroom and close the door, is what lies before you dreamy or frightening? The atmosphere in your bedroom can greatly affect your marriage. As you make your bedroom appeal to the five senses, you and your spouse will be drawn there. And the more you are drawn there, the more you will bring balance into your life and marriage. Some suggestions:

1. **Keep the purpose clear.** Most rooms in your home can be multipurpose. The master bedroom, however, is not one of them. Your bedroom's sole purpose should be for rest and romance. No matter how limited the space is in your home, make your bedroom a refuge.

2. **Make it fragrant.** Pleasant scents can put even the most weary bodies and souls into a wonderful state of mind. Skim through Song of Songs and you'll see how pleasant fragrances played a potent part in satisfying those love birds. Try it for yourself.

3. **Add a little luxury.** If you've ever ordered room service in a hotel, you know the pleasure this little luxury can bring. Dining in your bedroom can make even the simplest of food and beverage taste delightful and your marriage feel pampered.

4. **Play soothing music.** Every day you are bombarded with sounds. Most bring stress to your life. Make your bedroom a peaceful oasis of soothing sounds to help you turn off the outside world, relax, and unwind.

5. **Make it comfortable.** There's nothing like a good night's sleep in your own bed to get the rest you need. Consider a new mattress, a quilted comforter, giant pillows, or other accessories that make your bed irresistible.

6. **Turn out the lights.** This past New Year, I made one life-changing resolution that stuck. After reflecting on the areas of my life and our marriage that were out of balance, I realized the solution to most of the issues was simple—get a good night's sleep. So now I head to the bedroom by 9:00 p.m., take a hot bath, and am in bed by 9:30 to read and wind down for the day. Getting enough sleep has made me a new woman.

And my husband? Well, let's just say most nights he's not too far behind me when I head to bed.[9]

Sienese Painting
CENTURY
BAULE
MODERN WAR
LEGACY
THE SHOCK OF THE NEW
LEONARDO DA VINCI

CHAPTER SIX   SAFETY

comfort in uncertain times

The future will always be uncertain. While we may enjoy the illusion of safety, even in those moments, we're only a heartbeat away from eternity. That's why we must place our trust in God, knowing "Jesus Christ is the same yesterday and today and forever" (Heb. 13:8).

God hasn't lost control of our circumstances. He is our shield and defender—even when chaos rages around us. Isaiah 41:10 says, "So do not fear, for I am with you; do not be dismayed, for I am your God. I will strengthen you and help you; I will uphold you with my righteous right hand."

Now, more than ever, we should pray for and encourage each other daily. The writer of Hebrews reminds us, "Let us not give up meeting together" (10:25). We need to be nurtured spiritually through our churches and other fellowship groups.

We can find comfort in Scripture's promise that our heavenly Father cares about every detail of our life. In Matthew 10:29–31 TNIV, Jesus said, "Are not two sparrows sold for a penny? Yet not one of them will fall to the ground outside your Father's care. And even the very hairs of your head are all numbered. So don't be afraid; you are worth more than many sparrows." We can truly be confident about the future when we have this wonderful assurance.[1]

SAFE FOR LIFE

When my three children were young, I did everything I could to ensure their safety. But then they grew up, went to college, and moved away to other homes and cities where I couldn't supervise them. Yet because my children have accepted Christ, I know that regardless of what happens to them in this life, they are eternally secure. That's because God promises that when we accept Jesus as our Savior, we will not perish, but will have eternal life (John 3:16).

Once you know your eternal safety is sure, ask yourself what you've done to help others find that surety. It's a privilege and responsibility to tell others about God, about their sin, about their need to claim Jesus Christ as their Savior so their sins will be forgiven, and about heaven and how to get there. So pray, trusting God for the safety he'll one day provide you, and ask him to work on behalf of those who don't yet know him.[2]

I WILL LIE DOWN AND SLEEP IN PEACE, FOR YOU ALONE, O LORD, MAKE ME DWELL IN SAFETY. —PSALM 4:8

WORKING THROUGH TURMOIL

It was very hard to go to the White House on September 11, 2001. I was at home in Washington, D.C., the morning planes hit the World Trade Center in New York City, and I knew I had to get to work. But from all the reports I saw on television, Washington was under siege. It was one of those moments when I had to trust that God would be with me. That didn't mean God was necessarily going to protect me from terrorists or from death, but it did mean relying on his promise that he wouldn't ask me to do anything I couldn't handle without his help.

I think faith was also a great comfort and strength to the nation during that time. I helped organize the prayer service at the National Cathedral in the days following September 11, and I think that service helped calm, inspire, and remind our country that there is a God—and we can rely on him in times of fear and turmoil.[3]

O LORD MY GOD, I TAKE REFUGE IN YOU; SAVE AND DELIVER ME FROM ALL WHO PURSUE ME, OR THEY WILL TEAR ME LIKE A LION AND RIP ME TO PIECES WITH NO ONE TO RESCUE ME. —PSALM 7:1-2

finding peace as a hostage

Throughout their yearlong captivity by terrorists in the jungles of the southern Philippines, missionaries Martin and Gracia Burnham lived in fear, filth, and deprivation. They battled starvation, going as long as nine days without a meal, and struggled with depression caused by filthy living conditions. They had no access to a toilet. River baths were sporadic, and soap was hard to come by.

"Always I'd think, 'Things will get better tomorrow,'" Gracia says. "But they never did. It never got easier going to the bathroom on the jungle floor or being so filthy."

Yet, while circumstances didn't change, Gracia's perspective did. "You can't make peace, joy, and contentment just happen," she says. "The Holy Spirit has to do it, and he started to do it for me even as I struggled with disbelief and hatred because of our situation.

"I would go to the fire at our makeshift camp to get our food because Martin was almost always chained to a tree. I'd watch at the fire as we'd get shortchanged. The terrorists packed their bowls with rice while giving us a much smaller portion. Earlier, I had railed against the injustice. But now I was able to rejoice even in the small amount we received."

The contentment the missionaries experienced came through practice and prayer. "There were days when we would say, 'Lord, could you just show us that you love us?' Then something extraordinary would happen. One of the guys from Abu Sayyaf (terrorist organization) would decide to share some extra food with us, or a beautiful metallic blue dragonfly would pay us a visit. We thought of those things as the Lord saying, 'I'm still here.'"[4]

WHEN GOD TAKES THE REINS

THERE WE WERE: THREE WOMEN MISSIONARIES ON MULES WITH AN INDIAN GUIDE ON A SEVEN-HOUR RIDE INTO THE ANDES MOUNTAINS OF COLOMBIA, SOUTH AMERICA. WE WERE ON OUR WAY TO VISIT MISSIONARY FRIENDS WORKING IN A REMOTE VILLAGE IN THE MOUNTAINS.

They expected us to arrive around sundown, but because of several delays our trek did not begin until 4:00 p.m. We thought we could follow the trail with our flashlights.

Sooner than expected, our flashlights died. The blackness that surrounded us was almost palpable. I waved my hand in front of my face but could see nothing.

Without light, the mules refused to move. We pulled up their heads, prodded their sides, and slapped their rumps, but they wouldn't budge. We started to panic. We didn't know where we were, we couldn't go back, and we dared not dismount.

Our guide finally said, "Let go of the reins." That made no sense to us, but since we had no other recourse, we obeyed.

A marvelous thing happened. As we let go of the reins, each mule lowered its head and headed down the trail. We just held onto our saddle horns and sat still.

Overhead, a million stars blinked at us. They reminded us of God's wondrous power, assuring us that the Creator God knew where we were, even if we didn't. We began singing again.

Eventually we arrived at the village where our friends were staying. We paused and thanked the Lord for his guidance and safekeeping and then spent the night with our friends.

I remember that trip at times in my life when I'm at the end of my resources, strength, and abilities. I believe God allows dark valleys in the lives of his children so he can teach us to trust him. During those times, we don't know where we're going, we can't turn around, we can't get off the trail. Nothing happens because we're so tightly holding onto the reins of life, trying to force things to go our way.

God asks then that we simply let go and let him lead. As Psalm 46:10 says, "Be still, and know that I am God."[5]

SAFETY 59

Let the morning bring me word of your unfailing love, for I have put my trust in you. Show me the way I should go, for to you I lift up my soul. —Psalm 143:8

> SHOULD A FRIEND WHO SUSPECTS ABUSE APPROACH A WOMAN ABOUT IT?

SAVING A FRIEND FROM ABUSE

"Domestic violence has become an epidemic," says Brenda Branson, a former battered wife. The enormity of the problem, combined with the lack of skilled law enforcement officials and church leaders to address the problem, led retired police officer Don Stewart to write a book to help victims understand and flee from violence in their homes.

"Don offers hope to hurting women and presents a wakeup call to the Christian community to get involved," Brenda says. How can we tell if abuse is happening in a woman's life?

Don says that a batterer tries to isolate his victim. "If you see a woman being kept away from family, friends, or church, that's a red flag," he says. The second danger sign is a husband who constantly monitors his wife's whereabouts. "He may call her ten times a day at work, and if she doesn't answer each time, he demands to know where she was. If she doesn't arrive home in the evening at a precise time, he demands to know why."

Another red flag is a woman wearing pants and a long-sleeve shirt even when it's hot outside, or if she uses a lot of makeup. She could be trying to cover bruises.

Should a friend who suspects abuse approach a woman about it?

"It depends on your relationship," says Don. "If you're friends or even have a good casual relationship, invite her to breakfast or for coffee, and approach the subject gently by asking, 'Is everything okay? How is your relationship with your husband?' Don't condemn her or try to push her out of her relationship with her husband.

"At some point you need to say, 'I'm concerned about you. If you'd like to talk about anything that's troubling you, I'm here for you.' If she opens up, assure her that she isn't causing the abuse. Tell her: 'God doesn't approve of any man who beats, controls, or retaliates against his wife. Whenever you're ready to leave him, I'll help.'"

You might make an appointment for the two of you to sit down with a pastor, social worker, or law enforcement officer and decide where to go from there. If the woman is being abused but is unwilling to do anything about it, you might have to call the police for her. Reporting abuse is a difficult judgment call; it requires prayer and knowledge of the situation. But it may help save a woman's life.[6]

SAFETY 61

SAFE AT NIGHT

While it's good to be aware of your surroundings at all times, it's especially important for women to take precautions when it's dark outside. Here are a few stay-safe tips from the American Women's Self-Defense Association:

Park in well-lit areas or as close as possible to the front door of wherever you're going.

Keep your hands free to be able to fight off a potential attacker.

Walk with confidence so you don't look like an easy target.

Get some training in self-defense at your local community college or parks and recreation department.

Trust your instincts; if you feel threatened, immediately go to a well-populated or well-lit area.[7]

MEETING A GUY ONLINE

IT'S NOT HARD TO MEET A MAN VIA THE INTERNET, BUT IT IS HARD TO KNOW IF HE CAN BE TRUSTED. BEFORE YOU GET TOO CHATTY WITH YOUR NEW ONLINE FRIEND, FOLLOW THESE TIPS BY JESSE A. DILLINGER, A CHRISTIAN COUNSELOR:

1. Don't discuss personal problems—yours or his. This kind of talk can bring you to a deeper level of intimacy than you intend. Don't play counselor to his problems, either. Recommend professional help if the situation seems to merit it.

2. Don't discuss areas of vulnerability, such as: "My husband doesn't give me enough attention," or "I don't feel good about myself," or "I hate living where I live." A con artist will use those weaknesses to woo you, then use you.

3. Don't become dependent on hearing from this guy. Are you disappointed when you don't receive email from him? Are you beginning to fantasize about him? While he may seem far more sensitive and caring than your spouse or other men you know, in real life this guy may not pick up his socks, either.

4. Recognize that a con artist will tell you whatever he thinks you want to hear, and may be a good listener only because he's trying to find out all he can about you.

5. Never give out your phone number or address. Criminals can use this information for anything from credit card fraud to rape.

6. Screen names and photos can be deceiving. It's easy to scan a photo—anyone's photo—and claim that it is you.

7. Understand that just as you present only your best side via email, so does your online friend. He isn't about to tell you that he has a drinking problem or a criminal record. And you aren't telling him that your laundry pile now needs a ladder to access it.[8]

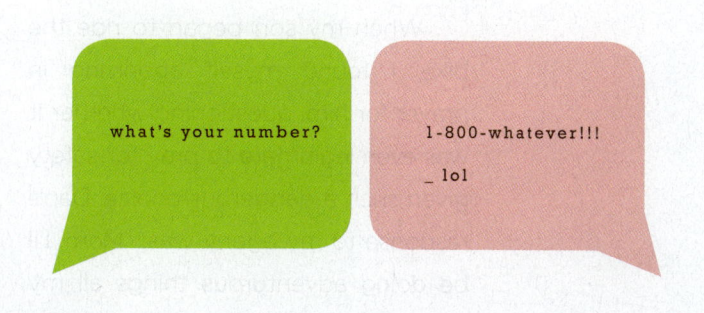

what's your number?

1-800-whatever!!!
_ lol

> I CONTINUED TO ASK FOR PHYSICAL PROTECTION, TOO, BUT CONCENTRATED ON INTERCEDING FOR SPIRITUAL PROTECTION.

DAN AND THE MOTORCYCLE

ONE DAY DAN, OUR HIGH SCHOOL SENIOR, DROVE UP IN A FRIEND'S VAN, AND TO OUR AMAZEMENT, UNLOADED A MOTORCYCLE. WE HOPED HE WAS JUST STORING IT FOR SOMEONE AND WERE RELIEVED WHEN HE SAID IT DIDN'T WORK.

But after some probing, we learned he had paid a hundred dollars for it and was ecstatic about his purchase.

Reluctantly, we allowed the bike to stay. It took a long time for Dan to repair the bike and get a license and insurance to drive it, since he had to finance all of that himself.

When my son began to ride the bike, I found myself agonizing in prayer for him, questioning whether it was even legitimate to pray for safety given such a dangerous choice. Dan's response to my agony was: "Mom, I'll be doing adventurous things all my life—hang-gliding, parachuting, hot-air ballooning. I'm always going to need your prayers for my safety." Adventure was in his blood.

One day, as I was praying about Dan and the bike, God put a new thought into my mind. It was as if he said, "You care so much about Dan's physical safety, and so do I. But do you care as much about his spiritual safety?"

I did care about Dan's spiritual well being, but I realized that my prayers weren't reflecting that concern. From that moment on, each time Dan got on the bike, I asked God to shield him from the dangers that could harm his soul. I continued to ask for physical protection, too, but concentrated on interceding for spiritual protection. Though I never really made peace with the bike, I realized that because of it, I was praying more than ever before for our son.[9]

KEEPING TEENS SAFE

Abduction is every parent's worst nightmare. But when it comes to preventing child abduction, knowledge is power, says Dr. Bunni Tobias, a licensed educational psychologist in Lake Forest, California. Here are Dr. Tobias's tips for helping your teens stay safe.

1. Listen to them. When your teens talk to you, stop what you're doing, make eye contact, and pay attention to what they're saying. This is not only a great way to keep informed on what your children are doing and with whom they're doing it, but it also shows them that you care about what they say and will be there to listen when bigger issues come up.

2. Affirm your child. One of the ways predators attract victims is by making them feel special. If your children already feel good about themselves, they'll be less likely to seek inappropriate attention from strangers.

3. Ask questions that open the door to awareness. Ask your children about something good that happened to them that day. Ask about something that frustrated or annoyed them. Did anyone make them feel uncomfortable or scared? Offer your child the vocabulary and the permission to talk about sensitive issues.

4. Discuss the dangers. A teen is old enough to know that the world is not always a safe place, but the child should also know what it takes to stay safe. Ask your kids what they would do if someone started following them. What would they do if they felt threatened or uncomfortable with an online friend? Talk through the options and create a solid plan to get through these situations.

5. Teach awareness. Use family trips, mall outings, even walks through your neighborhood to hone your children's observational and survival skills. Teach them to look around and really see the environment and people around them. Help them identify safe places to go to if they feel threatened or unsafe.[10]

CHAPTER SEVEN　LEAVING A LEGACY

the gift of financial order

My father died last year, less than twelve months after my mother died. It has been a challenging time of stress, sorrow, and sadness. But as I said at both of their memorial services, I have much to be thankful for. My parents set powerful examples of a loving marriage, admirable career choices, and whole-hearted commitment to family.

They also set a great example of financial preparation. Long before they died, Mom and Dad put their financial and medical affairs in order, easing my responsibility as executor of their estate. Before my mother was diagnosed with cancer and my father began having heart problems, they invited me to dinner and handed me a large envelope. It contained copies of their wills, their living wills, a list of what was in their safe-deposit box, and even a map of my father's office, identifying which papers were in what drawers.

After my mother's death, my father talked openly about their investments, gave me authority to write checks on his behalf, and included me in the process of checking his beneficiary designations.

The financial side of a person's life is not what matters most. It isn't the financial discussions I had with my parents that I'll always cherish; it's the conversations we had about their lives as well as other priceless moments.

But the financial side of life does matter. The longer a person lives, the more complex their financial situation becomes. Trying to piece it all together after an elderly person is gone can only add to the grief of their loved ones.

If it feels like a chore to pull some of these elements together now, perhaps you're not looking at it with the proper perspective. Try viewing the settling of your financial affairs as a legacy of love to your family.[1]

Charm is deceptive, and beauty is fleeting; but a woman who fears the Lord is to be praised. Honor her for all that her hands have done, and let her works bring her praise at the city gate. —Proverbs 31:30–31 TNIV

Transforming Guilt into Glory

I have had three abortions. Making this announcement never rolls easily off my tongue, nor does it become old hat. The last abortion occurred twenty years ago, but to this day I still experience pain, sorrow, resentment, and anger when I think of what happened. The abortions left such devastating scars that examining them plunges me into self-doubt and weakness.

Yet I've been cleansed through God's forgiveness and saved by grace. Daily I experience his loving touch. I turned to Christ after a friend gave me a Bible during a time of marital crisis. The marriage failed, but my faith grew, and God eventually blessed me with a Christian husband. Today, my life as a wife and mother of three is completely different from the life I led twenty years ago as a college student. Although I once used alcohol to numb the pain of the horrific decisions I made and to fill the emptiness I felt after my boyfriends abandoned me, I now find fulfillment in Jesus Christ.

I served in my church for years without speaking of the abortions, however. I intended to keep my shameful past a secret even from my husband, Steve.

But an event changed that thinking. I attended a meeting at which a crisis pregnancy counselor from another town spoke about pro-life work. She said that her pregnancy center needed someone to lead a Bible study to help women heal from past abortion experiences. At that moment a fog lifted. Right then and there, I confessed my abortions to the people in the room, then offered to be the one to lead women to a closer walk with God through Bible study.

I went home and told Steve what I had done. After his initial shock, he gave me his total support. I began to lead post-abortion Bible studies. Later I also became director of our crisis pregnancy center.

Being obedient to God's call has brought more blessings than I ever imagined. My ashes of grief have been transformed into a crown of beauty (Isa. 61:3).[2]

LEGACY OF LOVE

RECENTLY, MY MOTHER GAVE ME A STRAND OF BEAUTIFUL, HANDCRAFTED SILVER BEADS THAT SHE HAD PURCHASED ON A TRIP TO MEXICO YEARS AGO. SHE WORE THESE BEADS AGAINST A SOLID BLACK DRESS OR SWEATER, CREATING THE MOST DRAMATIC EFFECT.

My father once gave me a memoir he had written about his military service. Whenever I read it, I'm filled with love and pride. I will always treasure these keepsakes from my parents.

I am now searching for meaningful keepsakes to give to my own children. I don't have special jewelry, and I can't think of anything in my house that anyone would want. But I remember seeing a Bible at my friend Peggie's house that she was reading for a grandchild. I flipped through its pages and noticed handwritten notes in the margins. Peggie's love for her grandchild was written all over that Bible. Peggie said that while her friends were making quilts and creating needlepoint mementos for their grandchildren, she couldn't think of what to do.

"I wasn't good at any of those things," Peggie said, "but I love to read God's Word. That's when I got the idea to read a Bible for my children and grandchildren."

And read she did. I received an email from her that says: "I finished reading Bibles for my four grandchildren and my four children (two sons and their wives)."

Following Peggie's example, I bought a new Bible and read it in the course of a year while praying for my daughter Lauren and writing notes to her in the margins. For me this was a precious time to be in God's presence while focusing on my eldest child. I presented the Keepsake Bible to Lauren on her twenty-first birthday. I hope that when she reads this Bible she will know how much I love her. Now, I have begun reading a Bible for Lindsey, her sister.

I could give my daughters engraved jewelry, crystal, or a scrapbook made with love. But I can't think of a greater gift to give my children than God's Word—his gift to me of hope, love, and faith. And when they read my little notes and prayers in the margins, they will remember that I love them too.[3]

JOURNAL OF THANKS

You may have seen this journaling concept on The Oprah Winfrey Show, but no one has more to be thankful for than a Christian. There is a huge difference between feeling happy about your good luck and realizing that "every good and perfect gift is from above, coming down from the Father of the heavenly lights" (James 1:17).

I like to put a spin on gratitude journals by creating them for other people. There's nothing more meaningful for a leader or mentor than receiving a journal from a person they serve, outlining some of the ways they've seen Christ's love at work. Christian workers long to see fruit in the lives of those for whom they labor. Let your pastor or Sunday school teacher know how God has used their teaching and prayers to help you grow.

Whether you want to expand your prayer life, express your wonder at creation, give thanks, boost your faith, or trace God's work in the lives of your loved ones, there's a journaling style for you.

So forget any daunting notions of what a journal is supposed to be. And once you find a way to journal that feeds your relationship with God, stick with it and share your ideas with others.[4]

IF YOU DON'T HAVE A TON OF FREE TIME, A GRATITUDE JOURNAL IS EASY TO KEEP. ALL YOU HAVE TO DO EACH DAY IS LIST THREE TO FIVE THINGS FOR WHICH YOU'RE THANKFUL.

TURNING LOSS INTO CELEBRATION

I NEVER THOUGHT I'D MISS MY MOM'S TRADITIONAL GREEN-BEAN CASSEROLE. BUT THE FIRST THANKSGIVING AFTER MY FOLKS MOVED TO A RETIREMENT COMMUNITY IN FLORIDA, I FELT DOWNRIGHT NOSTALGIC ABOUT HER ANNUAL COVERED-DISH OFFERING AND ALL THE GOOD-NATURED TEASING ABOUT HER LIMITED CULINARY SKILLS THAT ACCOMPANIED IT EVERY THANKSGIVING. CELEBRATING WITH MY IN-LAWS JUST WASN'T THE SAME.

Traditions cement families. Rituals are packed with memories that communicate a family's story from generation to generation. Traditions tell family members that they're connected and have a shared history.

Some traditions stretch like a rubber band around the blessings of joyous transitions like a marriage or birth of a baby. But death, divorce, or any kind of loss can stretch cherished family traditions into an unexpected, unfamiliar shape. With some effort, however, we can transform those memories into something celebratory. As author Henri Nouwen writes, "Another step in turning our mourning into dancing has to do with not clutching what we have, not trying to reserve a safe place we can rest in, not trying to choreograph our own or others' lives, but to surrender to the God whom we love and want to follow."

A holiday may have become painful because of a loss, but it still contains the seed of something beautiful from the past that can provide balm for the present and begin to shape a new tradition for the future.

One grieving mother began a new tradition the year after her adult daughter unexpectedly died. Shortly before Christmas, the mother gave each family member money in a carousel tin (her daughter loved carousels) and the task of spending the money creatively to help someone in need. The next year during Christmas dinner, family members shared stories about how they had used the money. This new ritual provides the family with a way to remember their loved one in the context of new, life-giving memories.

Transition is a necessary part of life. It's an invitation to know at a deeper level the Savior who waits for us with celebration and a promise to one day wipe away every tear. You can navigate tradition during seasons of change with a bit of advance emotional preparation and some caring support.[5]

MY MOTHER'S FAITH

Mother died before my first birthday, leaving my dad to raise three daughters alone. I wanted to know everything about her, so as a child I hounded Dad with questions while he did farm chores.

I learned that my mother could look at a garment in a store window and sew one like it without a pattern. And when she baked pies to supplement the family income during the Great Depression, she was overwhelmed with orders.

I desperately wanted to be like my mother. I knew from her portrait I looked like her; we both had fair skin and bright blue eyes. But it was Mother's faith and attitude I most wanted to emulate. Mom refused to waste her life blaming others for hard times or unpleasant circumstances. Instead, she gave comfort and guidance from the Bible to those who were hurting. Mother's prayer life strengthened and encouraged her family and others. And when she was dying, she relied on her Lord's redeeming love to keep her daughters and their dad safe.

I've felt the effect of my mother's love and faith all my life. When I've been hurt in my marriage or career or when my children have been in distress, I've been keenly aware of God's Spirit giving me comfort and peace. I praise God for my mother's faith that continues to affect her family.[6]

Listen, my son, to your father's instruction
and do not forsake your mother's teaching.
They will be a garland to grace your head
and a chain to adorn your neck.
—Proverbs 1:8–9

model grandma

"MOM, YOU'RE GOING TO BE A GRANDMA SOON," MY DAUGHTER SAID. SHE AND HER HUSBAND WERE ECSTATIC AS THEY SHOWED US THE RESULTS OF A HOME PREGNANCY TEST. MY HUSBAND AND I LAUGHED, CRIED, HUGGED, AND CELEBRATED WITH THEM.

The next day it hit me. "I'm in my mid-forties. I'm too young to be a grandma!" I wondered what a modern grandma looked like. I asked God to show me what it meant.

The only grandma I recalled in Scripture was Lois, Timothy's grandmother. "Some role model," I thought. "There's only one verse about her." Two Timothy 1:5 calls Lois a woman of "sincere faith." The only other thing we know about her is that her name means "more desirable." "Desirable" didn't seem to fit the grandmother image. What's more desirable than being young?

Then a verse I'd memorized from Psalm 19 came to mind: "They are more precious than gold, than much pure gold; they are sweeter than honey, than honey from the comb" (v. 10). The verse referred to the Word of God and his commandments. That told me that to be like Lois, I needed to help my grandchild know Christ and make godly choices based on his Word and commandments. To model that for my grandkids would be a worthwhile goal for the rest of my life.

I now have two grandsons, Joshua and Nathanael. I love to share Bible stories and *Veggie Tales* videos with

> TO HELP MY GRANDCHILD KNOW CHRIST IS A WORTHWHILE GOAL FOR THE REST OF MY LIFE

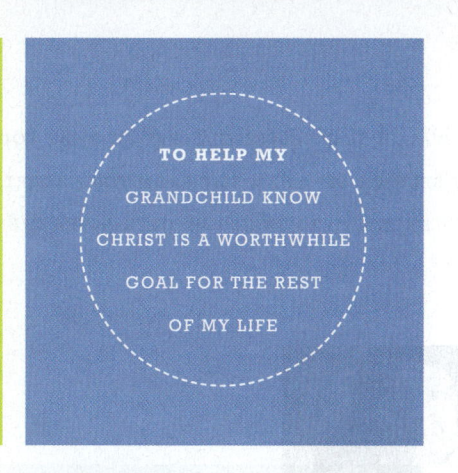

the toddlers. Josh, age two, enjoys praise music. When he hears a good song, he stops playing with his toys and leaps up to dance. Pointing to the carpet, he signals me to join him in the middle of our living room floor, and we do some lively arm waving and jumping around.

I pray constantly for these little ones. I've sung them Michael Card lullabies and, yes, have even had time to rock them to sleep. Prayer is already coming naturally to Josh. He bows his head as we pray before meals or bedtime. When Nathan gets an "owie," Josh tells his little brother that "Jesus will make it all right."

Someday in heaven, I'll introduce my grandsons to Lois and thank her for modeling genuine faith to Timothy. I'll tell her how much I appreciate her for being a woman who understood that it's more desirable to know Christ and his Word than anything else in the world.[7]

> I PRAY CONSTANTLY FOR THESE LITTLE ONES

LEAVING A LEGACY 73

ONLY BE CAREFUL, AND WATCH YOURSELVES CLOSELY SO THAT YOU DO NOT FORGET THE THINGS YOUR EYES HAVE SEEN OR LET THEM SLIP FROM YOUR HEART AS LONG AS YOU LIVE. TEACH THEM TO YOUR CHILDREN AND TO THEIR CHILDREN AFTER THEM. —DEUTERONOMY 4:9

TABITHA'S LEGACY

Tabitha wasn't famous; she probably wasn't even known outside her hometown. She didn't win any great awards or gain a high position, yet her life is recorded in Acts 9 to stand throughout all time. Why? Because she was faithful in doing what God had chosen her to do.

Tabitha was a disciple; someone who subscribed to Jesus' teachings and spread them not only by word, but by "always doing good and helping the poor" (v. 36 TNIV).

When I wonder what impact I'm making, Tabitha inspires me to continue doing the things the Lord has given me to do, such as helping someone clean house, babysitting a young child, or visiting a friend who's ill.

I also remember Paul's words in Galatians 6:9: "Let us not become weary in doing good, for at the proper time we will reap a harvest if we do not give up." As we're faithful in doing the little things, God may entrust us with bigger jobs.

In a time where many people are obsessed with themselves, courtesy and acknowledging the needs of others are becoming rare. Little acts of kindness can make us the salt of the earth. How different our world could be if we had more Tabithas.[8]

CHAPTER EIGHT **MONEY**

hope during unemployment

All through my husband's out-of-work nightmare, I prayed that God would provide for our family. But with each passing week, I wondered what was taking so long. Why isn't God answering any of my prayers? I thought.

I cried out to God again when I was rock-bottom desperate. Looking up out of my window as I waited for an answer, I noticed a flock of blackbirds glide across the clear blue sky. A familiar Bible verse came to me, as if whispered on their wings: "Consider the ravens: They do not sow or reap, they have no storeroom or barn; yet God feeds them. And how much more valuable are you than birds!" (Luke 12: 24).

I thought about the birds. And I began to look at my situation with fresh eyes. Then it struck me: God had been providing, all right. The reason I hadn't seen that before was because God's idea of provision is so different than mine. I had been waiting for God to provide my husband with a job. Instead, he had given us an opportunity to assess what was important. He had stopped us in our tracks to take a better look at ourselves and learn.

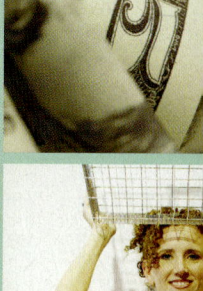

In these lean times, we have tightened our belts, done without frivolous things, and even done without things that are not so frivolous. I've watched our bank account drain away to dollars and change. At first dealing with that was painful, but now it's gotten easier. I'm grateful when I remember that we once had more than enough, and I look forward to the time when we will once more have more than we could hope for.[1]

THE MISSING CHECK

THIS WINTER WE DID SOME MAJOR REMODELING ON OUR HOUSE. THE PROJECT TOOK TWICE AS LONG AND COST TWICE AS MUCH AS WE'D FIGURED. ALL THE LITTLE PONDS OF MY CAREFULLY HOARDED SAVINGS DRIED UP, AND WE OWED SOME BESIDES. IT'S A SITUATION THAT WOULD HAVE MADE MY PENNY-PINCHING ANCESTORS VERY NERVOUS.

I responded to the overspending by drawing up a tight budget. No extra spending on anything until I got those savings accounts replenished and our debt under control.

Well, you guessed it: Along came an automobile insurance bill, a big one. I hadn't counted on it, and I had no idea how to pay it.

"Oh, no," moaned all those frightened voices of my past. "You shouldn't have spent all that money. Not even God can bail you out of this one."

The voices were wrong. When I balanced my checkbook, I discovered I had entered an amount into my ledger for a check I hadn't actually written. The amount was exactly what I needed to pay the insurance bill. How did that happen? In more than twenty-five years of doing the family books, I had never made a mistake like that before.

It felt like a lovely little miracle.

I believe that provision was God's way of assuring me that while saving and living without debt are all part of good stewardship, I don't have to make them my gods. The Living God will take care of me. I don't have to hoard and save, begrudging every dime I have to spend. I can count on the Lord as my provision.

After almost a century of worry in my family, I can begin to relax and trust God more than my own finagling.[2]

> **Trust in the LORD** with all your heart and lean not on your own understanding; in all your ways acknowledge him, and he will make your paths straight. —Proverbs 3: 5–6

GIVING BEFORE GETTING

Several years ago, we lost our business. Within four months, my husband went from being a respected banker with a great future to being completely unemployed and unsure of what to do next.

I blamed myself. Harold would not have left the bank if I hadn't pushed him to start a business. To his credit, Harold didn't blow up. But we still didn't talk about our money situation; we were too scared.

One day I fell on my face before God on the kitchen floor and just wept. I promised God that I'd do anything to get out of debt. Bible verses about stewardship came to mind, and I knew then that to honor God and get on the right track we had to give God a portion of our income—even while we were in debt—and that we had to start saving, too. If God ever blessed me with another dollar, I'd do things his way.

Ten days later, I got a phone call from a guy who offered me a job in commercial property management and sales. I took the job, worked hard, and God blessed my efforts. I began to make good commissions and built a clientele while Harold stayed home with the kids.

Three years later, Harold joined me in opening our own real estate company. But this time we gave to God first, saved a portion, then did everything we could to reduce our expenses and pay off our debts.

I was learning—the hard way—that God wants the first part of everything and that he blesses those who obey him. As a result of my experience, I'm convinced that giving to God and saving money are the antidotes for overspending. They produce a lasting feeling of well-being and satisfaction that spending can never satisfy long-term.

So many people believe that if they just have enough money, they'll be happy. But I say, folks, it's not going to happen. It's not how much you make; it's what you do with what you get that counts.[3]

ENOUGH FOR RETIREMENT

Surveys consistently show that only 4 to 7 percent of those who retire each year are financially independent. Other couples must depend on Social Security, relatives, welfare, or other charitable means to live. Poor planning is the primary culprit for this sad statistic. Conversely, good planning can make retirement some of the best years of your life.

Once upon a time, the average worker retired at age sixty-five and died at seventy-three. Planning for eight years of retirement was not hard. Between Social Security and a generous pension from a company for which you had worked over thirty years, your need for personal savings was minimal.

But times have changed. The employee who works for one company most of his life and earns great pension benefits is becoming an anachronism. Plus, average life spans are dramatically increasing.

To determine how much you need to save for retirement, first determine your retirement income needs. Assuming your house is paid for, a good rule-of-thumb is that you will require about 70 percent of your pre-retirement annual income to maintain your lifestyle. Multiply that amount by the number of years you expect to live beyond retirement.

What sources of income will be available to meet this need? Social Security will most likely be around in some form, so you can count on some income from it. A company pension is also a possibility, but, if you are like many of today's mobile workers, the pension may not be much.

The final source of retirement income is the one over which you have the most control: personal savings. One of the most important disciplines you can develop is putting a percentage of every paycheck into an investment account designed to provide you with income at your retirement.

If you are in your late thirties or early forties, you should start saving 15 percent of your income. Ratchet that up to 20 percent if you are in your late forties or early fifties and are just getting started.[4]

> AVERAGE LIFE SPANS ARE DRAMATICALLY INCREASING

> IN YOUR EARLY 40s YOU SHOULD BE SAVING 15% OF YOUR INCOME

NO ONE CAN SERVE TWO MASTERS. EITHER YOU WILL HATE THE ONE AND LOVE THE OTHER, OR YOU WILL BE DEVOTED TO THE ONE AND DESPISE THE OTHER. YOU CANNOT SERVE BOTH GOD AND MONEY. —MATTHEW 6:24 TNIV

THE BIG PICTURE ON GIVING

My lesson in humility began one Tuesday afternoon. Our son, Matt, sat perched on the steps of a downtown office building waiting for his father to pick him up. A man in shabby clothes ambled along, asking for money.

When Matt told me this story later, I felt my skin grow hot, thinking, *Yeah, right, he needed money for a tire. More like for drugs. Or a cheap bottle of wine.*

"The man said he needed seventeen dollars," Matt said. "So I gave him ten."

"Ten dollars?" I fumed. How dare this panhandler talk my son out of his hard-earned money? "Honey, why would you do such a thing?"

"Because it felt good to help somebody, Mom."

Ouch. Still, I felt Matt didn't understand the situation, didn't get the big picture about how the world worked. "A dollar would have been plenty, Matt. Just to show him you cared."

Matt's brow drew into a knot. "But wouldn't ten dollars show him I cared even more?"

Ouch again. Adult logic goes by the wayside when faced with a teen determined to do the right thing.

The Bible teaches that if your gift is giving, you should give generously (Rom. 12:6, 8). Then why wasn't I congratulating my son for being generous instead of chastising him for being taken advantage of by a stranger on the street?

He had done precisely as he'd been taught, not by me, obviously, but by Jesus: "Each of you should give what you have decided in your heart to give, not reluctantly or under compulsion, for God loves a cheerful giver" (2 Cor. 9:7 TNIV).

Matt wasn't a reluctant giver. But I was. He said yes to this needy man without feeling coerced. I would have said no and blamed the man for being pushy. My son was cheerful. I was infuriated.

Here's the saddest truth of all: I gladly write a check each December to a Christian mission for the homeless not far from the very spot where Matt did his kind deed. Sure, I'm willing to help the needy. But only if I control the amount and how it's spent. And only if I can drop my money in the mail, not press it into a grimy hand.[5]

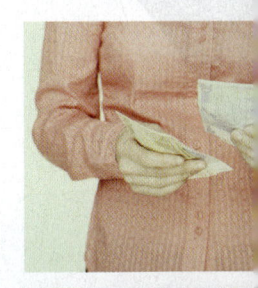

MONEY 79

a new approach to tithing

In the broad and widely asked question, "are we still required to tithe?" most christians agree that new testament writers insist that we be a giving, generous people (1 Tim. 6:18). So, at the very least, we must insist that believers today are expected to give generously.

Keep your lives free from the love of money and be content with what you have, because God has said, "Never will I leave you; never will I forsake you." —Hebrews 13:5

But how much should we give? Are we required by God to give 10 percent of everything we earn?

The following points may help focus the issue:

1. Beware of pride. There is a great spiritual danger in thinking that if in some area we have satisfied a specific, concrete demand, we have done everything that God requires. Ten percent is a lot of money to some folks; to others it's not very much. Isn't that one of the lessons to be learned from Jesus' comments about the widow's mite? (Luke 21:1–4). To suppose that God demands 10 percent—and nothing more—can foster a remarkably independent and idolatrous attitude: "This bit is for God, and the rest is mine by right." Likewise, if you choose to give more than 10 percent, you may become inebriated at the thought of your own generosity.

2. Remember why you're giving. A strictly legal perspective on giving soon runs into a plethora of complicated debates. Is this 10 percent of gross or net income? If we tithe on our net income, are we talking take-home pay only, or does it include what is withheld for medical insurance and retirement benefits?

It would be easy to list such questions for a page or two without ever asking, "How can I manage my affairs so that I can give more?" That is surely a better question than, "What's the correct interpretation so that I can do whatever's required and then get on with my life?"

Christians will want to acknowledge with gratitude that they are mere stewards of all that they possess. Moreover, New Testament ethics turn not so much on legal prescription as on lives joyfully submitted to God.

So, why not aim for 20 percent in your giving? Or 30? Or more, depending on your circumstances? "For you know the grace of our Lord Jesus Christ, that though he was rich, yet for your sakes he became poor, so that you through his poverty might become rich" (2 Cor. 8:9).[6]

THE JOYS OF LEANER LIVING

If you're dealing with less money at the end of the month, here are ways to trim your budget and find worthwhile lessons in the process.

1. Encourage each other. A person who is laid off from work may feel like a failure, especially when trying to provide for a family. That can lead to a cycle of depression and lethargy. My friend, Stephanie, faced this problem when her husband, Bill, was out of work.

Under the advice of their pastor, Stephanie urged Bill to create a budget for what money they did have. They found ways to save and be grateful for God's provision in the small things.

Bill also became great at saving money at the grocery store and actually cut the family's food budget in half. By saving in practical ways and encouraging each other, this couple weathered the storm until Bill was employed again. Their marriage was strengthened, they developed greater compassion for those in financial need, and they never forgot that contentment is a choice.

2. Adjust your expectations. When times are lean, change your definition of entertainment. Rediscover board games, enjoy a walk in a park, check out a new hiking trail. Instead of going out for dinner and a movie, consider going to a matinee or dollar theater and eating at home.

Update your wardrobe by shopping at a local consignment store. You can save as much as 40 percent on your clothing budget. If you have kids, swap their outgrown clothing with another family with kids in corresponding sizes.

3. Get your kids to help. Your kids may not go get jobs, but they can contribute to the family finances by shopping at garage sales and not complaining about the lack of expensive snack foods or pricey entertainment.[7]

> **HOPE THAT IS SEEN IS NO HOPE AT ALL. WHO HOPES FOR WHAT HE ALREADY HAS? BUT IF WE HOPE FOR WHAT WE DO NOT YET HAVE, WE WAIT FOR IT PATIENTLY.** —ROMANS 8:24–25

HOW I CURBED EXCESS SPENDING

I STARED AT OUR CREDIT CARD BILL IN AMAZEMENT. HAD I REALLY SPENT THAT MUCH MONEY LAST MONTH? I SIGHED AS I REMEMBERED MY NEW YEAR'S RESOLUTION TO SPEND LESS MONEY. LUKE 12:48 REMINDED ME, "FROM EVERYONE WHO HAS BEEN GIVEN MUCH, MUCH WILL BE DEMANDED."

Although our family wasn't rich, we did have more than many people in this world, and I knew God expected me as the bill payer in our family to manage our money responsibly. I realized I'd disappointed him by being a poor steward.

I decided things had to change. I had to pay off this credit card bill. But the deeper issue was my need to change a lifetime of bad financial habits. How could I stop my uncontrolled spending?

Through conversations with other women and time in prayer, I've discovered a great way to get my spending under control. I have to remove the temptation. For me, that means tossing out catalogs before I look through them. It means avoiding eBay and blocking the home shopping channels from my television so I don't accidentally see something I just have to have.

If you struggle with overspending, examine your spending habits to discover the ways you're tempted to spend. Then do your best to eliminate those temptations. You may have to steer clear of the warehouse club or the mall. Maybe you need to turn down invitations to home party shows, where you buy stuff just to avoid hurting the hostess's feelings. Wherever you're tempted to spend, look carefully for your way of escape.

To be honest with you, reducing spending is not always easy. I'm often tempted to spend with abandon. But by consistently focusing on removing the temptation, I've been able to curb excess spending and get on the path to reasonable financial management.[8]

CHAPTER NINE TRANSITIONS

becoming parents again

They were enjoying a carefree two teenage girls when Brenda and Chuck discovered they would be parents again. Here are their thoughts on making the transition to a late-in-life pregnancy.

Q. After you found out a baby was on the way, what steps did you take to adjust?

A. Brenda: Before we rushed into dealing with outside pressures, such as how our parents and family would react, we decided to prepare ourselves. We agreed that we weren't going to tell anyone about the baby until we were okay with the situation. We knew that we had to deal with the changes that were soon to come, and we trusted that God would make that okay for us.

Q. What were some challenges that you anticipated?

A. Chuck: The transition we would have to make from our established lifestyle to a new one was a major concern. Our daughters were fourteen and twelve, and we had a very relaxed schedule with them, allowing plenty of time for camping and vacationing. We knew some of that would stop, at least for some time. It took me a little while to adjust to the idea that we'd need to get back to a tight schedule again.

Q. How did this pregnancy affect your relationship?

A. Chuck: Even with all the pressures and adjustments of having a baby, the blessings far outweighed the stresses. Having a baby made us feel younger. Together, we had to focus on the task at hand. Instead of just thinking of our immediate, personal plans, we had to refocus on what we needed for the next twenty years. Our marriage became more youthful than it would have been otherwise.[1]

For this God is our God for ever and ever; he will be our guide even to the end. —Psalm 48:14

Nestling into the Empty Nest

I grieved each time one of our children left for college. I missed their physical presence. I missed having their friends around. I even missed things I thought I'd never miss: piles of junk in the front hall or the constant sound of music I didn't choose and didn't like.

Though some grieving is normal, I knew I had to make a choice in this life transition. I could continue to wallow in nostalgia and dwell on the past, or I could embrace the future.

As I prayerfully tackled this choice, I discovered a spiritual serendipity. Our empty nest provided me with more time for prayer. And as I spent more time with God, he transformed my attitude, changing the way I responded to this new season in life.

By the time Kendall, our youngest, left home, I had a better handle on my attitude. Instead of grieving this major milestone, I decided to celebrate freedom. My husband, Lynn, and I went to England with another couple. We rented a flat for a week in London, then checked into a bed and breakfast in the Cotswolds, where we leisurely roamed the countryside. On that trip, we slowly began to fine-tune our definition of family, rediscovering the priority of our marital relationship. That time together helped us focus on the exciting potential of a new phase in our lives.[2]

TRANSITIONS   85

lessons of a lay-off

ONE MORNING, AFTER RETURNING HOME FROM DRIVING THE KIDS TO THEIR CHRISTIAN SCHOOL, MY FRIEND SHERRY FOUND HER HUSBAND IN THEIR KITCHEN, WITH A SHOCKED LOOK ON HIS FACE.

Why are you home from work early?" Sherry asked, feeling her stomach tighten with dread.

"I've been laid off," he said. After ten faithful years as an aeronautic engineer, he was no longer needed at the plant.

As the family's financial stability and comfortable lifestyle began to crumble, so did Sherry's self-esteem. It wasn't long before their SUV and comfortable house had to be sold. Private school for their children no longer was an option.

It was a struggle, but over time, Sherry and her husband learned they could find happiness in simple living. Sherry also realized that the children's health, a stable marriage, and great friends were more precious than the stuff they had before her husband lost his job. She discovered that living on less really could mean more.

Not everyone fairs so well. My friend Stephanie's husband, Bill, was out of work for months. Mounting tension led to arguments, leaving both partners feeling defeated. Finally they went to their pastor for help.

The pastor urged Bill to create a budget for what money they did have. The couple found ways to save and be grateful for God's provision. By encouraging each other in the crisis, the couple weathered the storm until Bill was employed again. Their marriage grew stronger and they developed greater compassion for those in financial need. Most of all, they learned that contentment is a choice.[3]

FINDING WORTH AS A WIDOW

BECOMING A WIDOW CAN LEAVE YOU FEELING LONELY AND LOST. YOU'RE LONELY BECAUSE A LIVING PART OF YOURSELF HAS BEEN SEVERED FROM YOU, AND YOU'RE LOST BECAUSE YOU DON'T KNOW WHAT TO DO NEXT. YOU CAN'T VISUALIZE HOW THE REST OF YOUR LIFE IS SUPPOSED TO GO, NOW THAT THE LIFE YOU SHARED WITH YOUR HUSBAND HAS BEEN TAKEN AWAY. WHAT'S NEXT?

You expect the community of believers that surrounds you to offer you a role that is useful, honorable, and fulfilling. Instead, you're pushed together with other newly widowed singles and prompted to find a new mate, as if anything short of couple-life is deficient.

Christians desperately need to recover a way of seeing the single life as valid on its own terms, and not simply as a holding tank. Though never-marrieds are made to feel like failures, that would hardly be biblical. The apostle Paul, who was single, found his life so fulfilling that he said, "I wish that all were as I myself am" (1 Cor. 7:7 RSV).

Paul addressed the widow's situation as well, saying, "A [woman] is bound [to her husband] as long as [he] lives. But if the husband dies, she is free to marry anyone she wishes, only in the Lord. But in my judgment she is more blessed if she remains as she is" (vv. 39–40 RSV).

Remarriage is clearly permissible for people whose spouses die, yet Paul says that remaining single offers more happiness. In Paul's day, early Christians were hardly lonely, whatever their marital status. In close-knit church communities, mutual love was vivid evidence of Christ's presence, not just a pleasant, superficial fellowship. Few people led solitary lives.

Today there is so much cultural impatience with singleness that we can stand to load weight on the other side of the scale. Praise God that his grace is more than sufficient to see us through our bouts of loneliness. When we're feeling lonely, lost, or discouraged, we can look to the apostle Paul for encouragement.[4]

I've been thinking a lot about Sarah, Abraham's wife, these days. Genesis 12 says Abraham was seventy-five years old when he told Sarah, "Honey, pack up the furniture—we're moving" (vv. 4–5) Imagine Sarah (who was about a decade younger than her husband) gazing out of her kitchen window at her garden, waving to neighbors strolling by, rearranging a hanging plant, and thinking, this is my home, my community.

moving again

Next year maybe we'll expand the bedroom. Isn't life grand? Then Abraham comes in with his announcement.

I picture a stunned Sarah, shaking her head in disbelief and thinking, Where did you say we were going? We'll know it when we get there? Have you lost your mind?

I know how I feel about moving. In twenty-three years of marriage, my husband, Barry, and I have never lived any place longer than seven years. We've gone from northern Maine to southern Maine, then to Southern California, then south of San Francisco, then to the west coast of Florida, where we live now. I thought we had finally settled.

But we're moving again. As I write this, I'm staring at yet another transition, although this move is not as dramatic as the one that brought us all the way across the country. The truth is, I haven't completely thought through the move. I'm still at the "If I don't think about it, maybe it won't happen" stage. However, I do know this. If I do what is right and support my husband in his effort to lead our family, if I encourage him and respect him and pray for him as we make decisions, and if I don't give in to fear, I will be like Sarah, a woman whom God greatly blessed.

While I'm not crazy about moving, I'm warming up to the idea that it might not be so bad. I've done enough moving to know my heart eventually comes around. Besides, I decided a long time ago that I'd rather be in a tent in the desert with my husband than alone in a mansion. And if I go wherever my husband goes, even if he makes a wrong choice, I know I'm in God's will.[5]

TIPS FOR CHANGING CAREERS

HERE ARE MY **TOP TEN** SUGGESTIONS FOR MAKING A CAREER CHANGE LATER IN LIFE.

1. **Do a career assessment.** You can find tests for this online. Some of them are free and relatively simple. Others are multifaceted, and cost something. You can also find good career assessments through local counselors and colleges, making use of industry tests such as the Strong-Campbell Interest Inventory, Myers-Briggs for personality profiling, and Self-Directed Search.

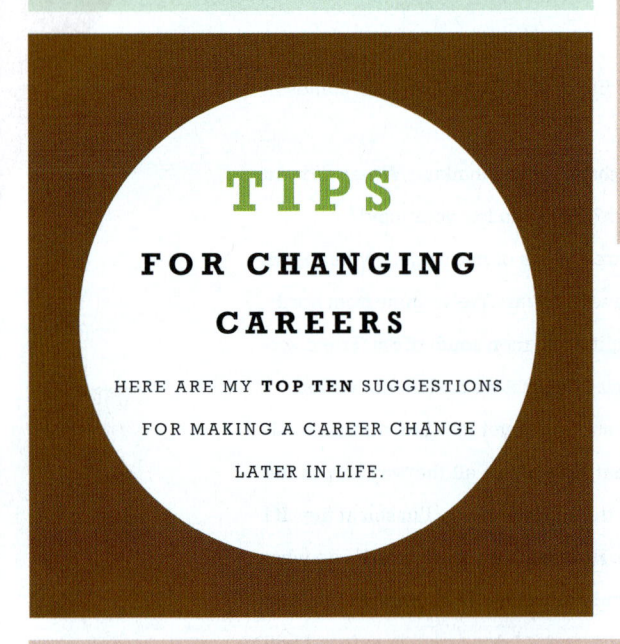

2. **Consult advisers.** Ask for input from select family, friends, fellow workers, career advisers, and experts. Ask them to describe your abilities, interests, personality, and values, as well as your blind spots. What kind of work do they think God has prepared for you?

3. **List your primary** life experience. Include education, work experiences, personal interests and hobbies, community and church activities. Circle what you did best and liked the most. Mark activities that were particularly rewarding.

4. **Network.** Whether exploring career direction or looking for a particular job, you need personal referrals. Your work experience and qualifications are enhanced by association with the person who referred you. So start making connections.

5. **Explore work options.** The Internet is great for exploring career opportunities of all kinds.

6. **Stay current.** Talent alone is not enough for many jobs today; knowledge and skill in changing technology is also required. So upgrade your skills, particularly in Internet maneuvering and software programs to remain employable. Keep learning.

7. **Reduce your debt load.** If your cost of living makes it hard to change careers, deal with the money issue. Wonderful resources are available to help you decrease your dependence on dollars and increase your freedom to change careers.

8. **Take courses on career planning & job search techniques.**

9. **Plan on working after retirement.** Forty-eight percent of retirees work at least part-time. Eighty percent of the soon-to-be-retiring baby-boomers plan on working beyond retirement age.

10. **Be optimistic.** Motivational speaker Zig Zigler writes that 85 percent of the reason people get jobs and get ahead in those jobs is a positive attitude. Exercise forgiveness to free you from hurts of the past, and practice loving others to overcome fear of the future.[6]

GROWING TOGETHER IN RETIREMENT

"I MARRIED YOU FOR BETTER OR FOR WORSE, BUT NOT FOR LUNCH." THAT OLD JOKE MAY NOT BE SO FUNNY WHEN YOU ACTUALLY RETIRE.

There are at least five major changes you may experience when you retire. Each offers you the opportunity to re-invent your marriage and enjoy time away from work.

1. Your identity changes. No longer is your identity linked with what you do, so sometimes it's difficult to know exactly who you are. This is a great time for you and your to develop some new interests.

2. You have more time together. Actually, you have the potential of spending twenty-four hours a day with your spouse. At first it may be awkward transitioning into being a couple again. In time you may enjoy the new closeness.

3. Your buffers are gone. Often a job and children deflect conflict and in-depth conversations with your spouse. Recognize this and learn to relate on a deeper level.

4. Communication changes. What worked well before may not work now. Voice mail messages or email with quick hellos and good-byes are no longer the primary way to reach your spouse. You actually have enough time now to start an argument and finish it.

5. Roles change. When you worked full-time, one of you had a major role in caring for the household, cooking meals, and so on. In retirement, those roles may need renegotiation.

Regardless of the change, view retirement as a great opportunity to deepen your understanding of one another.

You also have the opportunity and time to once more become intimate friends and lovers.

Reignite the spark of love. Jumpstart your dating activities. Enter your second childhood as you enjoy your grandchildren. Celebrate. Have fun.

Remember that marriage is a journey, not a destination, and you can decide where you want it to go in the future.[7]

Let the morning bring me word of your unfailing love, for I have put my trust in you. Show me the way I should go, for to you I lift up my soul. —Psalm 143:8

THE BIBLE ON RETIREMENT

When it comes to the concept of retirement, the Scriptures are silent. We know in the past people didn't live long enough to retire, but what about Abraham and Sarah or Methuselah? They lived well past age sixty-five.

Rather than focusing on the cessation of work, Scripture emphasizes that with age come wisdom and understanding (Job 12:12). Those are two precious qualities our world desperately needs today. So as Christian couples, what should be our attitude toward the post-job years when we typically have more time to call our own?

First, realize that retirement differs from couple to couple. Some people have plenty of resources such as money, health, and property so they can retire early and invest their lives in other activities. Others have few resources so they must continue to work well beyond the typical retirement age. However, every Christian couple has the privilege and responsibility of investing their lives in glorifying God.

So it seems only natural that a retired Christian couple will find new, creative ways to express God's love and service to those around them. Retirees may help an adult child who is in crisis or help out with the grandchildren.

Retirees Bob and Beverly moved to Vienna, Austria, to help organize the administrative office for a Christian ministry. Roger and Carol took early retirement, then joined the staff of their church. They're now helping to develop a model for ministering to marriages and families. Our retired neighbors, Bill and Fran, invest their time mentoring others, leading Bible studies, and directing a prayer ministry. These couples are only a few examples of how retirees can share their wisdom and understanding with others. Not one would describe themselves as retired.

Think about it. Do you really plan to retire? We don't.[8]

CHAPTER TEN PERSONAL GROWTH

keeping the dream alive
Wounded missionary Gracia Burnham waited on a wet, grassy mountainside. Moments before, she had been rescued from Muslim terrorists who had held her hostage, along with her husband, Martin, for more than a year in the dense jungles of the southern Philippines.

After more than a dozen failed attempts to rescue the hostages, Filipino soldiers successfully zeroed in on the terrorists. Gunfire erupted between the two camps. It was the seventeenth time Martin and Gracia had been caught in the middle of a rescue battle.

This time, the hostages were unable to escape injury. Gracia, shot in her right thigh, rolled to the ground and faked death. Martin, pierced three times in the chest, was fatally wounded.

Today Gracia is home in the United States with her children. Life is good but not yet normal. Gracia still finds herself waiting. "It seems like there are no normal days yet," Gracia says. "I miss being in the Philippines. You cook supper, you sit around, you go to bed. I loved that regular day."

In the meantime, Gracia has established The Martin and Gracia Burnham Foundation to raise money to train pilots and purchase airplanes to transport missionaries in remote locations in the world.

"With this foundation, my kids have seen how one person can make a difference," Gracia says. "Recently, my son said to me, 'Remember the times when we couldn't afford to go to the market in the Philippines, but we knew we were making a difference? Now we have this wonderful house. We never have to worry where our next meal is coming from. But are we making a difference?'

"I told him, 'Let's trust the Lord to help us do that.'

"So that's what I'm trying to do. Martin wanted others to know about Jesus and God's plan of salvation. And he was doing what he did best to make that happen. Martin had a dream, and the dream didn't have to die with him."[1]

SPEAKING OUT ON CORPORATE INFIDELITY

SIFTING THROUGH A BOX OF PERSONAL ITEMS FROM HER OLD OFFICE, SHERRON WATKINS, FORMER VICE PRESIDENT OF ENRON, CAME ACROSS A PAD OF STICKY NOTES TOPPED WITH A QUOTE FROM MARTIN LUTHER KING JR.: "OUR LIVES BEGIN TO END THE DAY WE BECOME SILENT ABOUT THINGS THAT MATTER."

"How many Enron employees had those pads sitting on their desks but didn't read the quote? Or if they did read it, didn't take it to heart?" Watkins asks today.

This wife, mother, and former executive at the energy giant Enron didn't stay silent about things that mattered. But little did she know that standing up for what was right would put her in the thick of one of the nation's most publicized corporate debacles that would cost Enron stockholders and employees millions of dollars and shake public confidence in corporate integrity.

Watkins grew up in a Christian home in Tomball, Texas, and became a believer while in grade school. At Salem Lutheran Church she learned that if you believe that God has your best interests at heart, it's a sin to worry. "Throughout my life, whenever I panic about something, I tell myself, 'I don't have to worry. I have to let this go. God has a plan.'

"This belief kept me anchored during my Enron odyssey."

Watkins's faith played out in the practical ways she conducted her business life, which proved crucial later when she blew the whistle on the company. "If I had cheated on my expense reports, for example, I wouldn't have felt I could meet with Ken Lay (former chairman and CEO of Enron)," Watkins says. "It turns out Enron tried to fire me, and I'm sure they looked through my expense reports to try to find some reason to do that.

"When you know you're going to be in heaven with your Maker one day, you think about doing what's right—not what you can get away with," Watkins says. "There's no hiding from God. That belief is what kept me from falling into a corporate culture that outwardly encouraged individuals to display respect and integrity while encouraging them to compromise whenever it was expedient."[2]

SHOW ME YOUR WAYS, O LORD, TEACH ME YOUR PATHS; GUIDE ME IN YOUR TRUTH AND TEACH ME, FOR YOU ARE GOD MY SAVIOR, AND MY HOPE IS IN YOU ALL DAY LONG.
—PSALM 25:4–5

FREEDOM FROM WORKAHOLISM

Christians are sometimes confused about God's perspective on work. How many of us have measured ourselves against the apostle Paul or other high, biblical achievers and thought, I'd better get moving! Compared to them, my work is nothing.

In truth, the Bible presents a different picture of work. Consider Jesus praising Mary for sitting at his feet rather than Martha for her compulsive serving (Luke 10:41–42). What about the apostle Paul's way of life? Night meetings were rare in a pre-electrical society. Instead, meals were shared by candlelight with family and friends. Long walks between towns provided time for exercise and fellowship. Sabbath observance was taken seriously. Clearly, work and ministry were valued along with worship, friendship, and rest.

Today, harried people are crying out for release from excessive work demands and values. Many Christians long for God's peace and a godly way of life. Precisely here, of course, the key question emerges: Is it possible to resist the frenetic workaholic culture that surrounds us?

As Christians we must remind each other time and again of God's good news for the workaholic. We worship a loving, faithful God who wants to free us from all enslaving idolatries, including excessive work.[3]

CONTROLLING ANGER

MY SONS WERE INNOCENT BYSTANDERS IN THE DRAMA THAT UNFOLDED THE NIGHT WE WERE WITHOUT POWER BECAUSE MY HUSBAND, STEVE, HAD FORGOTTEN TO PAY THE ELECTRIC BILL. MY ANGER PUT THE CHILDREN IN THE AWKWARD POSITION OF PLAYING PEACEMAKER FOR THEIR PARENTS.

Anger affects the people around you. It's human to take sides even when you're not involved. But to allow outside parties to be drawn into your anger is a cheap way to feed your ego and justify poor behavior.

I once watched two sisters-in-law let an argument over their small children turn into an ongoing dispute that separated a close family. Years later there's still division because the two women have drawn their grown children into the dispute.

Anger is usually a self-centered emotion. Your attention is turned inward on the wrong you've suffered. By contrast, the principle of selflessness is woven consistently throughout the entire Bible. We're taught to view others as more important than self (Phil. 2:3), and to die to personal desires as well as wounds (Matt. 16:24). Selflessness doesn't leave much room for anger.

To his credit, Steve never again neglected to pay the electric bill. He sincerely apologized once I became approachable, and time reduced the incident to what it should have been all along: a good-for-a-laugh story.[4]

CHAINS OF OPPORTUNITY

"If only I didn't have this troublesome kid." "If only I weren't married." "If only I didn't have to work." "If only I didn't have to do housework." "If only I weren't sick."

That's viewing commitments as chains. Paul rejects that kind of thinking. In the first two chapters of 2 Timothy, Paul attacks the word *ashamed* five times. He tells Timothy not to be ashamed of the Lord or of Paul, "his prisoner," but to join with him in suffering for the gospel, by the power of God (1:8). Paul says he is not ashamed of his suffering because of the grace of Jesus Christ. He also commends his friend Onesiphorus for not being ashamed of his chains (2 Tim. 1:16) and points out that the Word of God is not chained (2:9). Paul views limitations and weaknesses not as chains but as opportunities for God to shine.

Our challenge is to transform our attitude toward responsibilities as Paul did. Mothering, for example, may seem like a most limiting vocation unless we view it as a world-changing call. It's no accident that when Jesus defined greatness, he lifted up a small child. For all we know, in our mothering we might be raising another St. Augustine. His mother's piety and prayers had a profound influence on Augustine; he came to Christ as an adult and became a great leader of the Christian church.

No matter what your vocation, start thinking of your chains as opportunities to change your world, however limited, for Christ. Be like Paul, who was willing to "endure everything for the sake of the elect, that they too may obtain the salvation that is in Christ Jesus, with eternal glory" (v.10).[5]

He who began a good work in you will carry it on to completion until the day of Christ Jesus. —Philippians 1:6

SERVING WHERE CALLED

Years ago, when I discovered I had gifts that half the Christian church didn't think I should have, my husband, Stuart, encouraged me to use them. Once an interviewer on a radio show challenged him on that, saying, "You take the position you do on a woman's role in the church because of the wife you've got!"

My husband replied, "Has it ever occurred to you I have the wife I've got because of the position I take?"

Women should seek to use their gifts in ways that are acceptable to their community of believers. Ask God for guidance, and read as much as you can, then serve where you are called.

Personally, I believe I must answer to God for his gifts and calling on my life. I don't want to get to heaven and hear God say, "Half-done, thou half-faithful servant." Prayerfully I then exercise my gifts when I'm invited to do so and seek to use my strengths without being a stumbling block to others.

I don't believe women should bury their gifts or let anyone else bury them, either. There is a lost world of men and women waiting to hear what God's gifted women have to say to them. The eternal destiny of their souls may depend on it.[6]

FREEDOM FROM SECRETS

I DID SOMETHING STUPID AT ONE TIME, SOMETHING I KNEW WAS WRONG. I WANDERED INTO AN ONLINE CHAT ROOM AND FOUND MYSELF FLIRTING WITH A TOTAL STRANGER. MY MARRIAGE WASN'T GOING WELL, AND TO BE HONEST, THE ATTENTION THIS GUY GAVE ME FELT GOOD. BUT SIN, NO MATTER HOW GREAT IT FEELS AT FIRST, IS LIKE A LESION THAT DOESN'T HEAL. IT JUST KEEPS GETTING BIGGER UNTIL IT'S TREATED.

I needed the Holy Spirit's conviction and God's healing mercy. I received both, but not before my secret had turned me into a nervous wreck. I'd think, *What if someone finds out what I've done? What would they think of me?*

I know other women with secrets. Their secrets may not be exactly like mine, but the results are about the same. We become grumpy, anxious, stressed, or hurting as the harbored secret gnaws at us.

Sometimes the secrets we keep have to do with our mistakes. Other times, we harbor thoughts about wounds we've suffered at the hands of others. Either way—whether we're the villain or victim—our dark secrets can be potent sources of shame, pain, and bondage.

On the flip side, I've seen women experience freedom, healing, and joy when they've mustered the courage to tell others the secrets that have been keeping them hostage.

Being honest about my struggles and mistakes has made a difference in my life. The first time I told a close friend about my chat-room experience, I was pretty nervous. Now I talk openly about it to women's groups. I do it for the health of my soul and the integrity of my relationship with God. I also do it to help others come clean.

You and I will never be perfect. Most days we're not even good. If goodness and perfection were within our grasp, we wouldn't need Jesus. So we'll never be perfect this side of eternity. But we can be real. And we can live free of the chains of unspoken failures and wounds.[7]

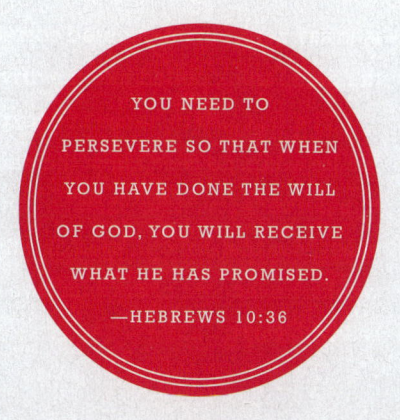

> YOU NEED TO PERSEVERE SO THAT WHEN YOU HAVE DONE THE WILL OF GOD, YOU WILL RECEIVE WHAT HE HAS PROMISED.
> —HEBREWS 10:36

PERSONAL GROWTH

CHAPTER ELEVEN **LOVE AND FRIENDSHIP**

rekindling romance

Ah, romance, that incredible attraction to the one you love. Where did it go, anyway? For some married folks, romance got buried under ten loads of dirty laundry piled in the hall.

Or romance fizzled when he started wearing black dress socks with denim cutoffs around the house. Or it died when you met him at the door; handing off the baby and a shrieking toddler, and saying you were out of there.

The longer you're married, the more challenging it becomes to keep romance sizzling.

Finding out what spells R-O-M-A-N-C-E to your partner means understanding what really makes him tick. One of the most romantic moments in my marriage was when my husband had a truckload of topsoil delivered as an anniversary present. Gardening is a major passion of mine, and Jeff knew I was frustrated with the hardpan clay that I couldn't coax into proper condition for my veggies and flowers. He had also overheard me pricing a load of topsoil and discarding the idea when I found out the cost.

Now, dirt is not a present you can brag about at the office. And Jeff has about as much interest in gardening as I do in his ongoing collection of Neil Diamond CDs. That is to say, zero. But he guessed correctly that I would light up like a Christmas tree when the dump truck pulled into the driveway.

There is also romance in unexpectedly lightening the mundane tasks of everyday life for your spouse. One of the dark secrets of my marriage is that I don't iron. So Jeff found it very romantic when he came home from a short business trip and found all his shirts immaculately pressed, lightly starched, and hanging in the closet. The next two weeks, he thought of me with love every morning when he pulled out a shirt that was ready to wear.[1]

TWO ARE BETTER THAN ONE, BECAUSE THEY HAVE A GOOD RETURN FOR THEIR WORK: IF ONE FALLS DOWN, HIS FRIEND CAN HELP HIM UP. —ECCLESIASTES 4:9–10

Lessons from My Pagan

"What's for lunch?" asked my husband, Steve, barely looking up from the couch. He sat unshaven late one Sunday morning, still in his bathrobe and watching a ball game on television.

I was miserable. Steve had no interest in my new faith in Christ and reacted to my church going as though I'd taken a lover. As he retreated into a hostile, quiet shell, I grew increasingly hurt and resentful, casting disapproving glances at everything he did.

We finally sat down to eat. I said a stiff prayer over dinner. When Steve looked up, he asked, "How was church?"

"It was wonderful," I said flatly. "You might have liked it if you'd been there." Another disapproving glance.

"I don't think so," he responded. After a long pause he added, "You know, if I were you, I'd feel pretty guilty."

"Guilty? Guilty?" I exploded, banging my fist on the table. "Why should I feel guilty? You're the one who is rejecting Christ!"

Softly, Steve delivered a blow from which I'd never recover: "Because, Virelle, I'm a pagan, and I'm behaving exactly as a pagan should. But you're a Christian, and you're not showing love."

For once, I had no words.

In my heart, I knew God agreed with Steve. I had been a pain to live with. I would burn with jealousy as I'd watch a Christian friend sit in church with her husband's arm around her. I'd seethe with self-pity as I heard other husbands pray aloud in a group. I justified my growing coldness toward Steve by viewing him as incapable of being the husband I now wanted. No longer being the wife he needed had never occurred to me. How could I possibly please God when I showed no love, gentleness, or grace to my husband?

The turning point came when I went on my knees that Sunday and prayed for forgiveness. I knew I had to change. God challenged me then to love Steve as if he were already the man I prayed he would become, whether it happened now, in ten years, or sometime after my death.

If faith is "being sure of what we hope for and certain of what we do not see" (Heb. 11:1), I had to believe that God would answer my deepest prayers for Steve in his own way, in his own time.[2]

LOVE & FRIENDSHIP 101

LIGHT FOR THE DARK TIMES OF MARRIAGE

WHEN KEVIN AND I MARRIED, I WAS A CHRONIC PEOPLE PLEASER. WHEN MY ATTEMPTS TO WIN KEVIN'S UNCEASING APPROVAL BY WEARING MY HAIR A CERTAIN WAY OR APOLOGIZING EVERY TIME I SENSED HE WAS ANGRY FAILED, MY PAINFUL EMOTIONS WERE ALMOST OVERWHELMING. FINALLY I TURNED TO GOD, WHO BECAME MY STRENGTH.

I eventually learned to care more about God's opinion of me than that of others. I may not have learned that lesson without suffering the seeming rejection of my husband. The more I sought God's approval during those dark days, the more Kevin softened toward me, and I toward him. We've both since learned how God can take a heart of stone and make it flesh (Ezek. 36:26). Those years of bearing with each other's weaknesses have made us more considerate parents, friends, and mates.

The Bible makes it clear that God wants people to stay married. Yet he hasn't made marriage particularly easy. When our vows are tested with sickness, poverty, or tough times, it's only by crying out to God in our inadequacy that difficult marriages can change and grow.

During our darkest moments, we are reminded by the psalms that God understands our situation and will help. In my marriage, the times that forgiveness has been hardest have also been the times I've experienced God's rewards in the most amazing ways. As Isaiah 64:4–5 says, "No eye has seen any God besides you, who acts on behalf of those who wait for him. You come to the help of those who gladly do right."[3]

SERVING YOUR SPOUSE

We serve God by serving others, particularly our spouse. God shapes us for service through a variety of methods, including using our spiritual gifts, our passions, our abilities, our personality, and our experiences.

God will also use the difficulties in your marriage to shape you into an effective minister to others. Who could better help the parents of a child with Down syndrome than other parents of a child with Down syndrome? Who could better help somebody deal with the pain of an addiction, a business failure, or a prodigal child than a couple who has been through these things and emerged with godly insights?

Could it be that the part of your marriage you most regret or resent and which you've wanted to hide or forget is the very thing God wants to use to help and encourage others who are sharing the same struggle? God doesn't just use our strengths; he uses our weaknesses and even our failures.

Marriage is a life-long process designed to teach you to see the needs of another person as more important than your own. It's a difficult transition because putting someone else above yourself is not natural. It's not instinctual for me to look at life from Kay's point of view, and it's not natural for her to look at life from my point of view.

To think of your spouse first requires an intentional shift that can be made only through the power of God in your life. As you and your spouse make that shift, your marriage will become more focused on the needs of others. The reward is greater than anything you could ever imagine.

God's plan for you and your spouse within marriage is wider and deeper than anything in your wildest, craziest dreams. May our heavenly Father help you to catch this vision as you chase it into the future.[4]

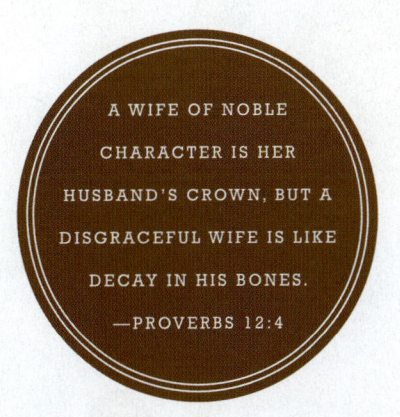

> A WIFE OF NOBLE CHARACTER IS HER HUSBAND'S CROWN, BUT A DISGRACEFUL WIFE IS LIKE DECAY IN HIS BONES.
> —PROVERBS 12:4

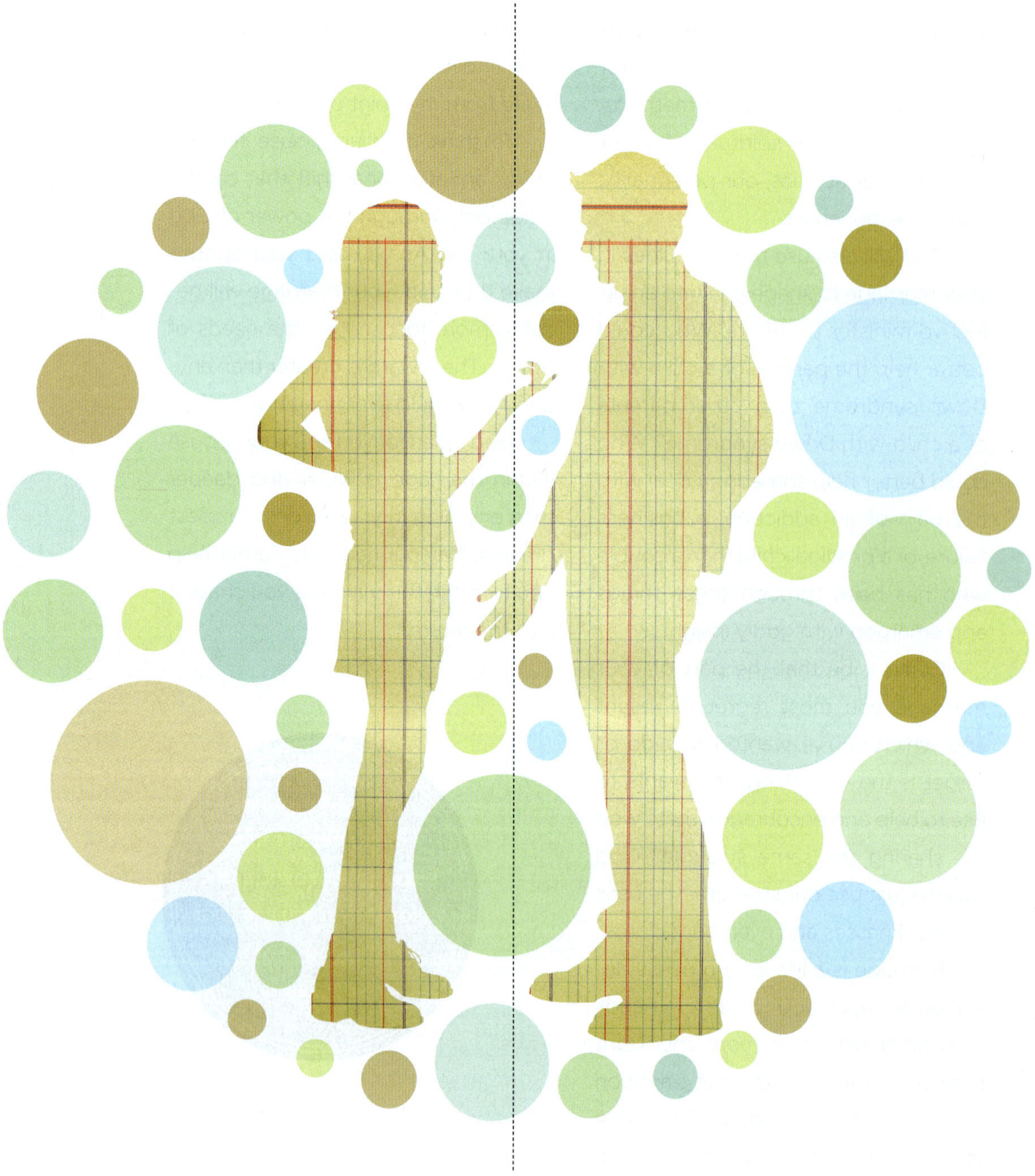

living with irreconcilable differences

My wife increasingly demanded that I listen to all the little details of her life. I really tried. Couldn't do it. For my part, I insisted that my wife go to a driving range with me and learn how to hit a golf ball. We ended that experiment ... after lesson one.

The more we tried to find areas of compatibility, the more miserable we became. I remember sitting on the bed beside Barbara after a failed sexual adventure (an activity at which we were no longer compatible, either, it seemed) and began mulling over all our differences: politics, kids, remodeling, attitudes toward in-laws, money, spirituality. The list was endless. I was overcome with a profound sense of how utterly different we were and how it was simply impossible for us to reconcile those differences.

But Barbara and I did agree on one thing: divorce wasn't an option. So we simply decided we were going to make this thing work despite our incompatibility. We didn't decide that in one day, and we didn't decide it with gusto. We simply felt we had no choice but to learn how to live with a person so utterly alien to us.

That's when we began to learn about martyrdom, about the death of the self, about giving up the desire for compatibility. If marriage wasn't about how my spouse could make me happier, we each concluded, then it must be about each of us trying to make the other one happier.

Here's the crazy thing: the more we stopped trying to get each other to be compatible, the happier our marriage became. Instead of our differences being insurmountable obstacles to happiness, they're what make our relationship interesting. Aggravating at times, to be sure, but ultimately more fascinating.

What's more, the more we've learned to love each other despite our differences, the more we've been able to love and serve those outside our marriage, most of whom are different from us in so many ways.

Certainly Barb and I share many things in common. But I doubt that we share any more than we do with anyone on the planet. Two human beings are going to share some things in common, no matter how different they are.[5]

LOVE & FRIENDSHIP 105

There is no fear in love. But perfect love drives out fear. —1 John 4:18

SPIRIT LIFTERS

If you'd like to encourage a friend but aren't sure what to say, mention her gifts and abilities. Ask yourself what would lift your spirits if you were in the same situation.

For example, I wrote this note to a young mother of four: "In case you sometimes forget, or in case you need to hear it today, I want to remind you that you're doing valuable, priceless, precious work, God's work, and he'll reward you for your faithfulness. He loves you and your special little ones, and he'll always keep you and them in his care." I enjoyed writing the note because I knew how I'd feel if I had received it.

Many of my notes are only a few sentences long. Some simply say, "I'm thinking of you today." You don't have to write a lengthy letter on expensive stationery. A short note on a pretty blank card, an art postcard, or a simple sheet of paper will do. If I find a recipe a friend would like, a magazine article that reminds me of someone, or even a sheet of stickers that my niece would love, I send it with a line that says, "This made me think of you. Enjoy!"

A warm smile and a cheery comment can make someone's day, but the written word, which represents an investment of the sender's time, however small, can repeatedly lift a person's spirits. In *The Power of Encouragement*, pastor David Jeremiah says, "Written encouragement comes directly from the heart, uninterrupted and uninhibited. That's why it's so powerful."[6]

KEEPING IN TOUCH

One of the most difficult things about moving is leaving behind close friends. You need to accept that some relationships you leave behind won't endure without the day-to-day touch points you had before. Grieve those losses, but realize that the flip side of this is that you get to ditch those difficult relationships you couldn't quite figure out how to get out of.

Here are some tips to keep friendship alive with people you've moved away from but still want to stay in contact with:

1. Express your love. Our tendency is to wall ourselves off from the pain of leaving. When you say good-bye to good friends, don't be afraid to cry and tell them how much you'll miss them.

2. Stay connected. My former college roommates and I rarely see each other. Yet, we stay connected by emailing each other about the big events in our lives.

3. Drop in. When we travel, my husband and I try to connect with friends at different places across the country where we've lived. It may be as simple as stopping by to say hello, or as involved as spending a weekend at a friend's home.

4. Redefine friendship. One of my friends at church was the music minister. She couldn't share many of her personal struggles with me then because my husband was one of the elders. Now that we've moved, she has the listening ear of someone who knows her situation but isn't actively involved in it.[7]

forty and single

SEVERAL YEARS AGO, SOME RESEARCHERS WITH FAR TOO MUCH TIME ON THEIR HANDS DISCOVERED THAT IF YOU'RE A SINGLE WOMAN OVER THE AGE OF THIRTY-FIVE, YOU MIGHT AS WELL CONVERT YOUR HOPE CHEST INTO A COFFIN BECAUSE YOU'RE OUT OF LUCK IN YOUR HUSBAND QUEST. ACCORDING TO THE STUDY, THE GOOD ONES ARE ALL TAKEN, AND EVEN THE BAD ONES ARE GONE.

Who asked for this advice, anyway? And who paid for that study?

We don't need researchers with government grants telling us we'll never marry. I happen to know the Master of all research and development, and he can change my marital status at any time.

Still, coming to grips with singleness has been an interesting process. I've learned to be content with being unmarried, even though that isn't what I would have chosen, particularly as I get older. But given the option, we don't always choose what's best for us, do we? Think of how many people bought a Yugo—how smart was that? In the meantime, God has blessed me with many special people who share my life. I wonder how many of those friendships I would have developed if I had married and had children.

"Fortysomething and Single" isn't the title I'd have chosen for this stage of my life. I'd have preferred "The Former Miss America," or maybe "Her Royal Highness." I still pray that God will allow me to add "Mrs." to my name. But whether or not that happens, I know the most important title I could ever gain is already mine: "Child of God." Nothing can take that title away, nothing can diminish it, and not even "Mrs." can overshadow it. I'm loved with a perfect love by the perfect man. I can't ask for more than that.[8]

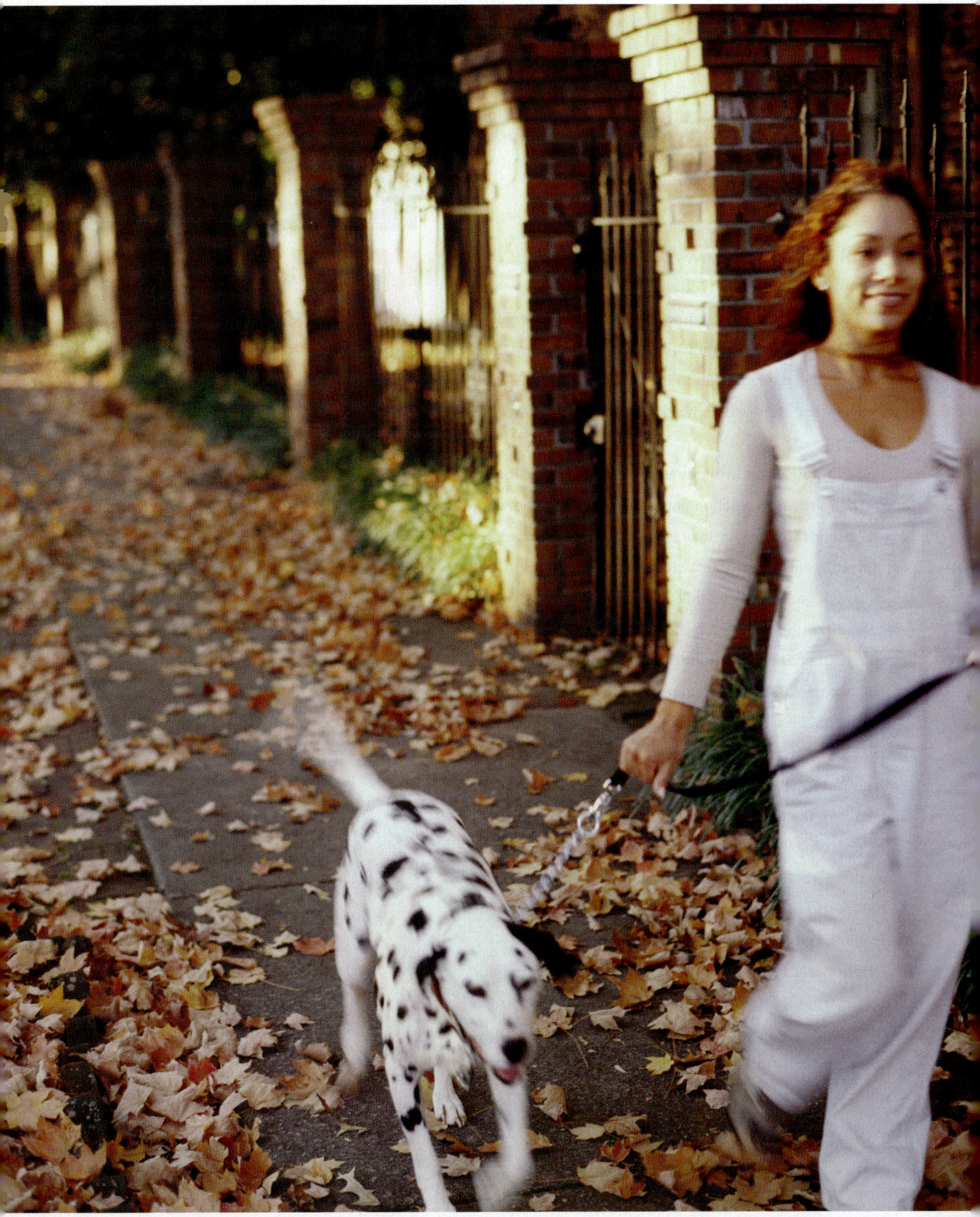

SHARING THE WORD

When I first heard about reading the Bible with nonbelievers, it seemed like a strange idea. I didn't think non-Christians would be interested in learning what Scripture says. But when I experimented with the idea, I was amazed by what happened.

Reading the Bible with my unbelieving friends fosters a level of spiritual interaction that falls somewhere between casual friendship and an invitation to church. It creates a comfortable environment in which others can begin to look at Jesus, ask questions, and talk about life issues.

Reading the Bible together also directly exposes people to the power of Scripture. The God who encourages, convicts, corrects, and sometimes bowls you over with his Word can do the same in an unbeliever's life. As God says in Isaiah 55:11, "My word that goes out from my mouth ... will not return to me empty, but will accomplish what I desire and achieve the purpose for which I sent it."

I don't know the details of what my friends are going through or what they are thinking, but God does. And I've seen him use Scripture to meet the needs of others, quell their fears, and dispel their misconceptions.

Hebrews 4:12 says, "For the word of God is living and active. Sharper than any double-edged sword, it penetrates even to dividing soul and spirit, joints and marrow; it judges the thoughts and attitudes of the heart."

Scripture can touch my friends' hearts in a way I may never be able to.[9]

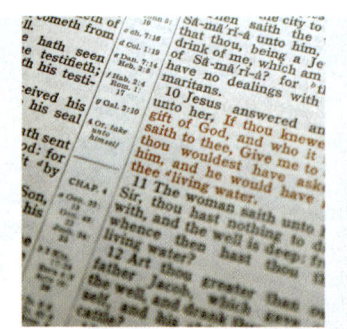

> I DON'T KNOW THE DETAILS OF WHAT MY FRIENDS ARE GOING THROUGH OR WHAT THEY ARE THINKING, BUT GOD DOES. AND I'VE SEEN HIM USE SCRIPTURE TO MEET THE NEEDS OF OTHERS, QUELL THEIR FEARS, AND DISPEL THEIR MISCONCEPTIONS.

COMFORT VERSES

MY FRIEND JULIE WAS GOING THROUGH A DIVORCE, BUT WE WERE SEPARATED BY HUNDREDS OF MILES. BECAUSE I COULDN'T SIT AND TALK WITH HER, I WROTE HER A LETTER OF ENCOURAGEMENT AND INCLUDED VERSE: "BUT THOSE WHO [WAIT ON] THE LORD WILL RENEW THEIR STRENGTH; THEY WILL SOAR ON WINGS LIKE EAGLES; THEY WILL RUN AND NOT GROW WEARY, THEY WILL WALK AND NOT BE FAINT" (ISA. 40:31).

I spoke with Julie many times after that, but she never mentioned my letter, and eventually I forgot about it. Three years later, we met for lunch. As Julie was recounting the ups and downs of her failed marriage she said, "Anna, I've read the verse you sent me every day. There were many days when I don't think I would have made it without that verse."

I sat in silence, awed by God's work through a single verse of his Word. Up until then I'd felt helpless in comforting Julie, but now I realized that by sharing Scripture I'd given Julie the one thing that was able to boost her confidence and carry her through her dark days.

So many people around us are hurting. Some need comfort or release from fear, while others need confidence to face difficulties. Do you want to give someone a double blessing? The next time you hear of someone in need, prayerfully select an appropriate Scripture and include it in the card or letter you send. The friend will love hearing from you, and God's Word may be just what she needs to keep going.[10]

CHAPTER TWELVE FAMILY

burden of blessing

A few years ago, my father found my mother on the bedroom floor. She had fallen while making the bed. Her collarbone snapped when she fell, which was not surprising given her combined ailments: Parkinson's disease and osteoporosis.

Something else appeared to have broken in my mother as well, however. Confused and fearful, she took to wandering from room to room at night, looking for intruders. My father, who was eighty and profoundly deaf, felt helpless to deal with my mother's rapidly deteriorating condition.

My husband and I moved back to Texas to help care for my parents. I have since become an expert at reading medical bills, insurance claims, and Medicare statements. My parents had helped us prepare for their deaths. What we hadn't prepared for was their decline. Many nights I lie in bed wondering how much longer my father's precarious health and strength will hold out. What will I do when it doesn't? My parents' resources are not sufficient enough to hire round-the-clock nursing. I remember how my mother cared for her dying parents, and I think of how no one in our family has ever lived or died in a nursing home.

I have many questions about the future. But I have learned not to repeat that cliché that perpetuates our idolatry of independence: "I don't want to be a burden to my children."

Throughout our lives, we are a burden to others. From the moment of conception, we are nourished and nurtured by others. The load we lay on others only becomes more visible as we age. The truth is that, should I live another twenty years, I will be a burden to my spouse or my children or the state, if not all of them. So what I most want to learn is not how to live longer, or even how to live a healthier or more productive life, but how best to be a burden. One that might also be a blessing.[1]

Blessed are those who fear the Lord, who find great delight in his commands. Their children will be mighty in the land; the generation of the upright will be blessed. —Psalm 112:1–2 TNIV

Intrusive Mother-in-Law

Q. *My husband recently took over the family business. My mother-in-law takes care of the books. But now that she knows all about our finances*, *she thinks she can tell us how to spend our money. I'm fed up. Help!*

A. Criticism by a mother-in-law cuts deep. And if she has inside information on your finances, the cut is even more likely to hurt. However, you have a few options to curtail the unwelcome critique of your financial decisions.

First, because this is a new working dynamic, your husband might still have a window of opportunity to find a new position for your mother-in-law that removes her from bookkeeping without hurting her feelings. Take your mother-in-law's personality and abilities into consideration when determining whether she would respond well to a job change.

If such a move would create a larger problem than the one you currently deal with, the second option is to set clear boundaries. When your mother-in-law offers her opinion about a financial decision you've made, be polite but assertive. Don't feel obligated to explain or apologize for your choices; simply say something non-defensive like, "You think so, huh?" Even better, completely agree with her. Say something like, "You're probably right. Thanks for the input." You may cringe at this, but it works. In time she'll back off.

Another option is to create a diversion by asking her questions, such as, **How was money handled in your home when you were a child? How about in your marriage?** Explore how and why she handles money the way she does. You have to do this with a genuine heart, however, with the purpose of understanding her, not to argue a point.

The bottom line is that you have to do something before you get even more fed up and say something you regret.[2]

ADOPTING AS A SINGLE MOM

FIVE YEARS AGO, AT THE GUATEMALA CITY AIRPORT, I WAS HANDED A BABY WRAPPED IN A BLANKET. I PEELED BACK THE LAYERS AND SAW THE MOST BEAUTIFUL BABY I'D EVER SEEN. I KNEW WITHOUT A DOUBT THAT MY JOURNEY TO GET HER HAD BEEN WORTH IT.

When I was growing up, I dreamed of getting married and having children. But after I married the man of my dreams, my fairy-tale romance turned into the shocking reality of an unfaithful husband. After six years of marriage, my husband told me he didn't love me anymore and left.

It seemed the years I'd spent waiting to become a mom were in vain. But some time later, God prompted me to take a giant leap of faith and adopt a child. While I had a heart for a Hispanic child, I wanted to be open to God's direction, so I prayed he would make it obvious where my child should come from. As I met with an adoption specialist, it became clear that the only country that met my requirements and that was willing to allow a single woman to adopt was Guatemala.

LaShay was almost seven months old when I first held her. She was petite but had the most adorable roundness. I had prayed for a happy, healthy, well-adjusted baby so the transition would be easy for her and for me as a single mom. And God answered that prayer.

As the years have flown by, I've continually seen God's hand on our lives. I have a wonderful daycare that's a source of strength and caring. With no spouse to call upon in case of emergencies or even to give me a break so I can run errands or have a night off from cooking dinner, I rely on the Lord and the love of my friends and family, who constantly keep me in prayer. Although my family lives out of state, we stay connected through lots of phone calls, letters, packages, and visits. Their loving support gives me strength through the ups and downs of parenting.[3]

NO MORE CHILDREN FOR ME

"So when are you going to have another one?"

For a long time, that was a painful question for me to answer. Now that I'm over forty and my daughter, Miriam, is a teenager, I'm more often asked: "Do you have any other children?" The answer still catches in my throat: "She's the only one."

I've spent the last fifteen years brushing off the subject of having more children with a shrug, a lighthearted comment, or a curt remark, while fighting back tears. Before I had Miriam, I went through a variety of fertility treatments, so my husband, Joe, and I were thrilled to finally hold Miriam in our arms. We figured our infertility problems were over.

We were wrong. We staggered through more treatments, this time bearing the medical expenses on a single income, since I had quit my job to stay home with our daughter. Finally we decided to stop. Because we still longed for another child, we pursued adoption. But that didn't work out.

I am one of more than a half million women in the United States who are experiencing the heartbreak of reproductive failure. I have secondary infertility.

I wish I could say that after all these years, I have gotten over the pain of being unable to have more than one child, but I know I have not. Just recently, I experienced a sharp pang of envy when the only other family I knew dealing with secondary infertility adopted two little girls. I worked through that pain, confessing my jealousy and receiving God's comfort, but I had to slip out of the baby shower when I began to cry. I was happy for the adoptive parents, but incredibly sad that adoption was out for us.

Meantime, God gently prods me to keep moving forward. When I lament that others have what I want, I falter in running the course that God has set before me (Heb. 12:1, 2). So to keep from stumbling, I firmly hold on with one hand to the One who gave his life for me, and with the other hand lightly grasp another gift he graciously bestowed upon me—my precious daughter.[4]

MY SISTER AND FRIEND

I was seven the year my sister Jody was born. I treated her like a doll, taking her for walks in the stroller, changing her clothes at random, and even dropping her occasionally. I called my sister Josie after one of my favorite cartoons, Josie and the Pussycats. When she entered kindergarten, I was the teacher's aide for her class. I wrote letters from Santa to her and her classmates. When I went away to college, Jody faithfully wrote me the funniest letters I'd ever read. They were so hilarious that I started reading them to friends while we waited for classes to begin. The crowd of listeners grew until Jody discovered what I was doing and started randomly inserting words like tampon in the text to embarrass me out of reading the letters aloud.

When I got married, Jody was learning to drive. When she finally went to college, she moved in with me and my husband and son. During the years she was renting a room from us, our friendship really grew. Obviously we'd always been sisters, but the difference in our ages hadn't really allowed us to be buddies.

I came to realize that Jody and I are the most alike of all the kids in our family. We even look so alike that people have asked if we're twins. Today we're both adults and live less than a mile apart. We have similar careers (I'm a writer who sometimes edits; she's an editor who sometimes writes), we have many of the same hobbies, and we volunteer in the same children's ministry at the same church.

When we chat by phone, we realize we're both making the same thing for dinner. I guess we're on the same wavelength. Jody and I spend so much time together that our husbands tease us about going through withdrawal if one of us goes out of town for a few days.

I've discovered a drawback to having such a close sister, though. It's easy to take her for granted. Jody has shown me how important it is to remember to send cards, bring chocolates, or treat each other at the movies. Even the closest sisters in the world need to show each other that they're special.[5]

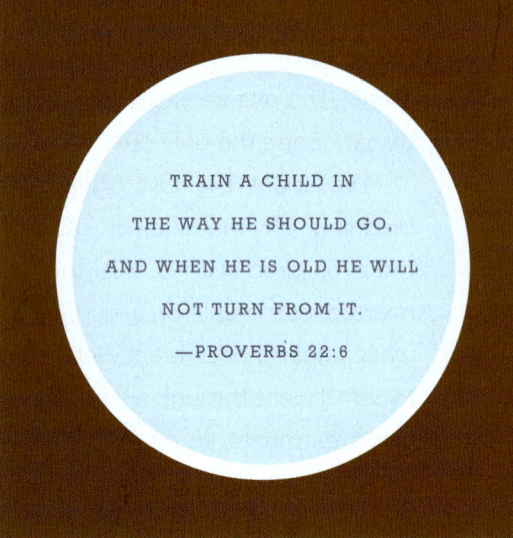

> TRAIN A CHILD IN THE WAY HE SHOULD GO, AND WHEN HE IS OLD HE WILL NOT TURN FROM IT.
> —PROVERBS 22:6

LESTER'S GAME

MY YOUNGER BROTHER LESTER DIED SUDDENLY AND UNEXPECTEDLY. IT WAS A DIFFICULT AND TRYING TIME; HOWEVER, AT HIS FUNERAL I MET MANY OF HIS WORK ASSOCIATES WHO ALSO LOVED HIM. SEVERAL PEOPLE MENTIONED THE GAME THAT LESTER HAD BEEN DEVELOPING.

For Lester, word games were a way to both educate minds and build community. I knew about his game and had played it with him several times. I had bugged him for years to complete the concept and put it into something for others to play. Now it seemed that I was the one who would have to fulfill his dream.

When my sisters and I cleaned out Lester's apartment, all the parts and pieces of the game came home with me. Later that year, our daughter and son and their families came to spend the holidays with us. On the last night of their visit, we brought down all the game parts from our attic and spent time looking through the boxes more carefully. We found work that represented thousands of hours of Lester's efforts. There were two game boards that he had developed as well as paperwork showing which one was his favorite.

There also were rough drafts of rules of play and ten folders of words with definitions already categorized and leveled for difficulty. Our son-in-law, who is an artist by birth and a printer by trade, offered to produce twenty-five games for our family if I would choose the words, type them, and e-mail them to him. I did that. Today, Uncle Lester's games can be purchased from catalogs and via the Internet.

My brother Lester was a simple, but brilliant, man who loved people and loved the Lord. I think he would have been proud to see the fruits of his labors now available for everyone to enjoy.

My love for my brother, and a compelling push from God, helped me work to see this dream accomplished. I thank God for his faithfulness in helping us realize Lester's vision, and I pray that many people will experience my brother's contagious love and faith through playing his games.[6]

FAMILY 117

taking my daughter to college

I forget who warned me not to blink. But I now realize he knew what he was talking about. As I drove home from Holland, Michigan, to Chicago that warm August afternoon, I was blinking again. This time I was blinking back tears on a three-hour drive that seemed to take twice as long. I had just deposited my firstborn on the steps of a dormitory.

Train a child in the way he should go, and when he is old he will not turn from it. —Proverbs 22:6

Now I began making withdrawal after withdrawal from a memory account I had opened eighteen years before. It seemed like only yesterday that I had driven my bright-eyed, black-haired baby girl home from the hospital, snuggled in her car seat next to her mother. I think my eyes were leaking that day, too.

Okay, I'll admit it. It wasn't the first time I had gotten a lump in my throat and had to reach for the tissue box. That also happened when my baby began to exercise small steps of independence. I remember her first babysitting job. Her first date. Her first job at camp that took her away from home all summer. But somehow dropping her off at college was the hardest blink of all.

After I got home, I couldn't resist the urge to go into Kristin's bedroom and think about why I missed her so much. She wouldn't be around for our regular family nights munching popcorn and watching family vacation videos. She would be absent from our pew at church. I wouldn't be able to holler at her for tying up the phone line. I would miss her availability to drive our middle daughter to youth group on Wednesday nights and to help our youngest daughter get dressed up for Halloween.

It has been four years since that tearful good-bye at Hope College, and my perspective as a father has changed. I am more convinced than ever how brief life is. Years blur. Time moves at bullet-train speed. Opportunities pass that can never be recaptured. Unfulfilled plans form a pile of gnawing regrets.

I now understand in a new way why Moses asked God to coach him on how to number his days to help him lead his people wisely and finish with the fewest number of falls (see Psalm 90).[7]

LIFE IS **brief**

NUMBER YOUR **days**

FAMILY 119

making new traditions

I'VE ALWAYS LOVED FAMILY TRADITIONS. WHEN OUR CHILDREN WERE YOUNG, I PULLED THE SAME DECORATIONS OUT OF STORAGE EVERY THANKSGIVING, CHRISTMAS, VALENTINE'S DAY, EASTER, AND FOURTH OF JULY.

We celebrated in traditional ways, too. Though the number of faces around our Thanksgiving table varied each year, our family of five formed the nucleus of this celebration of feasting. We spent the day preparing food. We got out the fancy white tablecloth, good china and silverware, and the kids made place cards for our guests.

I dreaded our first Thanksgiving without the kids because I feared their absence would magnify the emptiness of this new season of life. So we accepted an invitation from friends, and for the first time in twenty years, I didn't cook a turkey. I anticipated withdrawal symptoms, but to my surprise, I enjoyed the freedom from responsibility. Now my husband, Lynn, and I look forward to finding new ways to celebrate, such as serving turkey to the homeless at our church, or taking a cross-country ski trek. In that we thank God not only for food but for the blessing of his creation.

On our first Valentine's Day as empty nesters, we realized that going out for dinner alone was no longer unusual. So we invited a single mom to share dinner with us at home. Our first Mother's Day and Father's Day alone also felt a bit odd, so Lynn and I began to honor each other for the role we played in our children's lives, instead of depending on them to set the pace.

As we learn to hold our children more loosely, we're growing closer as a couple and opening ourselves up to what God has in store for us in the future.[8]

Though the number OF FACES AROUND OUR THANKSGIVING TABLE VARIED EACH YEAR, OUR FAMILY OF FIVE FORMED THE NUCLEUS OF THIS CELEBRATION OF FEASTING.

PARENTING A PRODIGAL

Parents of rebellious children desperately want their kids to straighten out their lives and fear the outcome if they don't. These parents often also find their marriages or personal lives being torn apart by guilt and blame.

Marriage and family counselor H. Norman Wright, the author of more than sixty books, knows first hand the corrosive effect of a prodigal child on a marriage. For four years, Wright and his wife, Joyce, watched and prayed for their daughter, Sheryl, as she stumbled through progressively more destructive stages of rebellion.

But they fought the temptation to blame themselves for what was happening. "Every parent is imperfect; we're going to make mistakes," Wright says. "But you need to remember that you could be the most perfect parent in the world. You could have done everything according to Scripture, and that child still might choose the wrong path in life. Look at God, the perfect Father. He created two perfect people, and they both turned their backs on him and rejected him."

However, if parents have failed in any way (and what parent hasn't?), Wright recommends honestly admitting the mistake and accepting responsibility for it. He then advises listening to 2 Corinthians 7:10, which says, "Godly sorrow brings repentance that leads to salvation and leaves no regret."

"This means we don't have to live with regrets in our life. We can be free from that," Wright says.

It's easy for parents of prodigals to get overwhelmed by their child's negative behavior and no longer see good in that child. That's a big mistake, Wright says. He encourages parents to focus on their child's positive qualities, even at the height of their rebellious behavior, and to praise the child for them.

If you're having trouble finding positives in your prodigal, Wright suggests answering these questions: **What good qualities could you see in your child before he/she rebelled? What good things has her teacher or pastor said about her? What positive qualities have your relatives pointed out about him?**

"Look for ways to encourage the child, to believe in the child," says Wright. "You could say, 'I don't agree with what's going on, but I believe in you and I value you and I love you.' This puts pressure on a prodigal and makes him uncomfortable, but inwardly the child values it."[9]

ENJOYING ADULT DAUGHTERS

WHEN MY THREE DAUGHTERS WERE YOUNG, I NEVER DREAMED THEY'D EVENTUALLY BECOME MY FRIENDS. ALTHOUGH IT TOOK THIRTY-SOME YEARS, IT WAS WORTH THE WAIT. TODAY MY DAUGHTERS KNOW ALL ABOUT ME AND LOVE ME ANYWAY. THEY ASK MY ADVICE, OFFER EMOTIONAL SUPPORT, AND LISTEN WHEN I TALK. THIS IS FRIENDSHIP AT ITS BEST.

Here are some ways to nurture friendship with your adult daughters:

1. Keep an open mind. As we discuss ideas from various angles, we're challenged to learn from each other.

2. Be a good listener. I cultivated this habit when my girls were young because being listened to is critical for self-esteem and a close relationship.

3. Remember. It's easy to expect maturity equal to our own in someone else. Remembering the struggles I had as a thirty-something helps me understand some of the difficulties my daughters are having.

4. Look for ways to show love. We do nice things for friends outside the family, but sometimes we forget those closest to us. A small gift or card, lunch out, or an offer to baby-sit are all ways to say you care.

5. Be open about feelings. When one of my daughters felt emotionally abandoned by me, she waited several months to let me know how she felt. I regretted having put her through that pain, and I wished she had told me about it sooner.

6. Respect each daughter's uniqueness. Your daughters won't always do things the way you do or believe as you do. Strive for understanding rather than correction.

7. Be quick to forgive. We often hold onto resentments against family members long after we would have forgiven the same hurts from outsiders. Let Ephesians 4:32 NASB be your guide: "Be kind to one another, tender-hearted, forgiving each other, just as God in Christ also has forgiven you."

8. Pray together. Recently I was nervous about a speaking engagement, but my fears subsided after my girls prayed for me. When one of them was helping a friend through a marital difficulty, I prayed for her and her friend.[10]

ENDNOTES

Ch. 1

1. Beverly J. Porter, "Makeover with a Mission," *Virtue* (December 1998/January 1999).

2. Margaret Feinberg, "Makeover Mania," *Today's Christian* (September/October 2004).

3. Liz Curtis Higgs, "Fearless at Fifty," *Today's Christian Woman* (November/December 2004).

4. Kim Alexis in "Beyond Beauty," *Today's Christian Woman* (July/August 1999).

5. Joanna Bloss, "Flex Appeal," *Today's Christian Woman* (September/October 2005).

6. Nancy Tester, "A Novel Idea," *Today's Christian Woman* (January/February 2005).

7. Ronna Snyder, "Managing Menopause," *Today's Christian Woman* (March/April 2005).

8. Elizabeth Moll Stalcup, "Does Prayer Heal?" *Virtue* (December 1998/January 1999).

9. Karen Scalf Linamen, "Surprised by Depression," *Marriage Partnership* (Fall 2000).

10. Phyllis Ten Elshof, "Taking on Breast Cancer," *Today's Christian Woman*, (March/April 2002).

Ch. 2

1. Cheri Fuller, "The Busy Woman's Guide to Prayer," *Today's Christian Woman* (March/April 2004).

2. Lauretta Patterson, "Need Hope?" *Virtue* (October/November 1998).

3. Phyllis Ten Elshof, "Taking on Breast Cancer," *Today's Christian Woman* (March/April 2002).

4. Constance Fink, "You've Got Prayer," *Today's Christian Woman* (July/August 2005).

5. Rachael Phillips, "Are You Too Busy for God?" *Virtue* (April/May 1999).

6. Joanna Bloss, "Feeling Spiritually Dry?" *Virtue* (December 1999/January 2000).

7. Lauretta Patterson, "Need Hope?" *Virtue* (October/November 1998).

8. Julie-Allyson Ieron, "A New Church Home," *Today's Christian Woman* (July/August 2005).

9. Sue Brockett, "Following God's Lead," *Today's Christian Woman* (January/February 2004).

Ch. 3

1. Lauren F. Winner, "In Today's Culture, What Does It Mean to Keep the Sabbath Holy?" *Today's Christian Woman* (January/February 2004).

2. Lauretta Patterson, "Need Hope?" *Virtue* (October/November 1998).

3. Ruth McGinnis, as told to Amy M. Tatum, "Discovering a Healthier You," *Today's Christian Woman* (September/October 2002).

4. "How to Get a Good Night's Rest," *Today's Christian Woman* (March/April 2005).

5. Sheila Wray Gregoire, "When Sleeping Together Drives You Apart," *Marriage Partnership* (Summer 2002).

6. Verla Gillmor, "Working 9 to 5," *Today's Christian Woman* (November/December 1999).

7. Christy Varney Pierce, "The Workaholic Christian," *Regeneration Quarterly* (January 1, 1996).

8. Karen Scalf Linamen, "Unplugged!" *Today's Christian Woman* (March/April 2001).

9. Teresa Turner Vining, "The Recipe for Peace," *Today's Christian Woman* (March/April 2001).

10. Terry Willits, "Summertime Fun," *Marriage Partnership* (Summer 2002).

Ch. 4

1. Marlee LeDai, "Go Girl!" *Today's Christian Woman* (September/October 2005).

2. ibid

3. ibid

4. Lori Roeleveld, "News You Can Use," *Today's Christian Woman* (January/February 2005).

5. Sheila Wray Gregoire, "Tune Off and Tune In," *Marriage Partnership* (Spring 2003).

6. Holly G. Miller, "Love That Vacation Feeling?" *Today's Christian Woman* (July/August 1999).

7. Jane Heitman, "Party Time!" *Today's Christian Woman* (September/October 2000).

8. Rachael Phillips, "Going My Way?" *Marriage Partnership* (Summer 2005).

Ch. 5

1. Lonni Collins Pratt, "Hospitality," *Virtue* (December 1998/January 1999).

2. Lauren F. Winner, "Sabbath and Strangers," *Books and Culture* (March 1, 2000).

3. Wendy Lawton, "Perfect Presents," *Virtue* (December 1999/January 2000).

4. Jymette Seager, "A Country Garden Faire," *Virtue* (June/July 1999).

5. Lesa Engelthaler, "The Neighborhood Project," *Virtue* (June/July 1999).

6. ibid

7. Martha Wolowicz, "Joy in the Night," *Virtue* (August/September 1999).

8. Terry Willits, "Good, Clean Fun," *Marriage Partnership* (Spring 2003).

9. Terry Willits, "Bedroom Priorities," *Marriage Partnership* (Summer 2001).

Ch. 6

1. Shirley Dobson, "In God We Trust," *Today's Christian Woman* (January/February 2002).

2. Anne Graham Lotz, "In God We Trust," *Today's Christian Woman* (January/February 2002).

3. Karen Hughes, as told to Corrie Cutrer, "No Place Like Home," *Today's Christian Woman* (November/December 2004).

4. Corrie Cutrer, "Soul Survivor," *Today's Christian Woman* (July/August 2003).

5. Ruth Rodger, "Led Through Total Darkness," *Today's Christian* (May/June 1998).

6. Brenda Branson and Don Stewart as told to Corrie Cutrer, "The Silent Epidemic," *Today's Christian Woman* (September/October 2004).

7. "Stay Safe After Sundown," *Today's Christian Woman* (March/April 2002).

8. Jan Brown, "How to Be Wise About Men Online," *Today's Christian Woman* (November/December 1997).

9. Carol Savage Plueddemann, "On Two Wheels and a Prayer," *Marriage Partnership* (Winter 1992).

10. "Safe Keeping," *Christian Parenting Today* (Fall 2003).

Ch. 7

1. Matt Bell, "One Final Gift," www.ChristianityToday.com (September 28, 2005).

2. Laurie Westlake, "The Cost of Confession," *Virtue* (August/September 1999).

3. Austine Keller, "Creating a Keepsake," *Christian Parenting Today* (Winter 2005).

4. Jody Veenker, "Are You a Journaling Dropout?" *Today's Christian Woman* (May/June 2004).

5. Michelle Van Loon, "The New Normal," *Today's Christian Woman* (November/December 2005).

6. Laverne Chapman, *Virtue* (December 1998/January 1999).

7. Sharon Colwell, "Kindred Spirits," *Virtue* (June/July 1999).

8. Kathleen Borrasca, "Kindred Spirits," *Virtue* (June/July 1999).

Ch. 8

1. Laurie Jackson, "Laid Off!" *Today's Christian Woman* (July/August 2004).

2. Wynne Gillis, "A Surprise from Heaven," *Virtue* (February/March 1999).

3. Mary Hunt as told to Linda Piepenbrink, "Why It Pays to Be Cheap," *Today's Christian Woman* (May/June 1998).

4. Scott Kays, "Are You Ready for Retirement?" *Marriage Partnership* (Winter 2000).

5. Liz Curtis Higgs, "A Cheerful Giver," *Today's Christian Woman* (November/December 2003).

6. D.A. Carson, "Are Christians Required to Tithe?" *Christianity Today* (November 15, 1999).

7. Ellie Kay, "Living on Less and Loving It!" *Today's Christian Woman* (July/August 2002).

8. Katrina Baker, "Surviving the Splurge," *Today's Christian Woman* (January/February 2003).

Ch. 9

1. Janine Petry, "Unexpectedly Expecting," *Marriage Partnership* (Winter 2000).

2. Carol Kuykendall, "Celebrating the Empty Nest," *Virtue* (October/November 1998).

3. Ellie Kay, "Living on Less and Loving It!" *Today's Christian Woman* (July/August 2002).

4. Frederica Mathewes-Green, "Widowed and Lonely," *Today's Christian* (July/August 2005).

5. Nancy Kennedy, "Honey, Start Packing — We're Moving!" *Virtue* (October/November 1998).

6. Brian Ray, "Contemplating a Career Change," www.FaithInTheWorkplace.com (October 20, 2004).

7. David and Claudia Arp, "Five Ways Your Marriage Changes When You Retire," *Marriage Partnership* (Winter 2000).

8. David and Claudia Arp, "How Christian Is Retirement?" *Marriage Partnership* (Winter 2000).

Ch. 10

1. Corrie Cutrer, "Soul Survivor," *Today's Christian Woman* (July/August 2003).

2. Julie-Allyson Ieron, "Taking On Enron," *Today's Christian Woman* (September/October 2004).

3. Christy Varney Pierce, "The Workaholic Christian," *Regeneration Quarterly* (January 1, 1996).

4. Mayo Mathers, "Anger Management," *Today's Christian Woman* (January/February 2004).

5. Mitali Perkins, "The Picture of Greatness," *Virtue* (June/July 1999).

6. Jill Briscoe, "Does the Bible Really Say I Can't Teach Men?" *Today's Christian Woman* (November/December 2003).

7. Karen Scalf Linamen, "Psst … I've Got a Secret," *Today's Christian Woman* (September/October 2001).

Ch. 11

1. Cindy Crosby, "Some Enchanted Evening!" *Marriage Partnership* (Fall 2000).

2. Virelle Kidder, "When He Doesn't Believe," *Today's Christian Woman* (May/June 2001).

3. Dawn Yrene, "When Marriage Gets Tough," *Marriage Partnership* (Fall 2004).

4. Rick Warren, "The Purpose-Driven Marriage," *Marriage Partnership* (Summer 2004).

5. Mark Galli, "Irreconcilable Differences — So?" *Marriage Partnership* (Winter 2004).

6. LeAnne Benfield, "Noteworthy," *Today's Christian Woman* (July/August 2004).

7. Cindy Crosby, "New Girl in Town," *Today's Christian Woman* (January/February 2002).

8. Dee Gray, "Still Single," *Today's Christian Woman* (January/February 2002).

9. Laura T. De Gomez, "Back to the Bible," *Today's Christian Woman* (November/December 2004).

10. Anna Edwards, "Send the Word," *Virtue* (October/November 1999).

Ch. 12

1. Virginia Stem Owens, "What Shall We Do With Mother?" *Books & Culture* (July 1999).

2. Leslie Parrott, "Money-Minded Mother-in-law," *Today's Christian Woman* (September/October 2005).

3. Melissa Montana, "A Dream Fulfilled," *Today's Christian Woman* (November/December 2004).

4. Penny Schlaf Musco, "Secondary Infertility," *Today's Christian Woman* (March/April 2001).

5. Amy Nappa, "Sister, Sister," *Today's Christian Woman* (July/August 2000).

6. Ruby Hovda, "My Brother's Legacy of Joy," *Today's Christian* (November/December 2005).

7. Greg Asimakoupoulos, "In the Blink of an Eye," *Christian Parenting Today* (Fall 2005).

8. Carol Kuykendall, "Celebrating the Empty Nest," *Virtue* (October/November 1998).

9. Caryn D. Rivadeneira, "Married, with Prodigals," *Marriage Partnership* (Summer 2000).

10. Barbara Smith, "My Daughters, My Friends," *Virtue* (October/November 1999).

Encouragement
for your busy life.

With *Today's Christian Woman* magazine you'll enjoy the inspiration, insight, and much needed laughter that bring balance to your challenging days.

From cover to cover, *Today's Christian Woman* is brimming with inspiring features and compelling stories that bring biblical perspective to your busy life and help you live out your faith. Lively articles on family, career, children, health and friendships fill every issue.

And best of all, there's NO RISK!

Let *Today's Christian Woman* refresh and encourage you! Start your RISK-FREE trial subscription today!

Also, Download New Survival Guides for Women at TodaysChristianWomanStore.com

christianitytoday.com/go/tcwmag_dv

At Inspirio we love to hear from you — your stories, your feedback, and your product ideas. Please send your comments to us by way of e-mail at icares@zondervan.com or to the address below:

Attn: Inspirio Cares
5300 Patterson Avenue SE
Grand Rapids, MI 49530

inspirio

If you would like further information about Inspirio and the products we create please visit us at:
www.inspiriogifts.com

Thank you and God bless!